1

Beloved, Be LOVED!

By Garry Glaub

Table of Contents:

Dedication:

Beloved, if God so loved us, we also ought to love one another.
1 John 4:11 (NKJV)

This book is dedicated to my sister, Julee Weems, who has suffered with Lyme's disease for the last eight years. Some people with Lyme's seem to receive treatment early and not see the far-reaching effects that Julee has endured, and continues to endure. As a professional musician, the tremors in her hands have made it impossible to play the guitar or flute, so those of us who love to hear her play have also suffered in the process. The associated tremors have made the simplest tasks in her life nearly impossible. Through it all, she has reached points of sadness and frustration, but is holding onto her hope! It is difficult to imagine how I would handle it if those aspects of my life that were most important to me were gone. I guess we may all face that eventually, as we age, and the fact that our bodies decline is a part of this broken world. But Jesus reminded us when He left earth that He went to prepare a place for us. That place will have no tears, no pain, no illnesses or diseases, and best of all, no sin! Everyone who reads this, please pray for Julee. She has the softest heart for Jesus, and her faith has impacted my faith deeply! Watching her in this process has taught me more about my faith, too. Do we really believe what we claim to believe? When all around us is going smoothly, faith in God and in God's promises are much easier than when all we have to stand on are His promises. We never know God is all we need until God is all we have. In the darkest places, we come to realize that God is everything. Betsie Ten Boom, sister of Corrie, said this when in the Ravensbruck Concentration Camp, where she died during World War II:

"There is no pit so deep, that God's love is not deeper still."

Thank you, Lord, for my precious sister. Thank you, Lord, for putting this book on my heart. May it glorify You in every way, for You alone are worthy. In the name of Jesus!

Preface:

Simply by turning on the radio, we can listen to an almost infinite number of songs about love. After all, "love is all you need." Are we really willing, "to climb the highest mountain or swim the deepest sea," to demonstrate our love, or do we change partners more frequently than we change shampoos? Contrastingly, country songs seem to focus more on lost love. We all know the adage that, "it is better to have loved and lost than never to have loved at all." The reason that love is such a common theme in so many songs is that love is a common need and concern for all who live. John Donne correctly stated that, "No man is an island," as the desolation of loneliness leads to suicidal thoughts and actions. Yet we sometimes forget that being alone is far better than being with someone who despises us. It is difficult to fathom anyone arguing with the fact that we need love, both to give and receive, and this does not seem to be learned behavior, but this desire for love is completely innate. A newborn baby immediately cries for love and attention, and those needs do not dissipate over time. We all seem to be on paths to find love, but are there different kinds of love? Some people seem to put a much higher priority on the physical expressions of love than on love itself. To most others, love is more of a mathematical equation than a feeling or emotion. "I will love you, if you will do A + B +

C!" That "if" completely changes love, though, and in a very limiting manner. Love is more than a feeling; it is a way of life!

Conditional love is not even a close relative of unconditional love. Most of us likely could give examples of unconditional love in our own lives. For me, my dog has been one of the best examples. She loves me no matter what I do and no matter how I smell; the size of my salary does not affect her, nor does the size of my house; she really does not care at all how I look or what I wear; but she loves me for who I am, who I was and who I will be! Parenthood is another example of unconditional love, to many. In fact, the birth of a child can completely change people.

Yet each person ever born has the best example of unconditional love in God our Creator. To correct a misconception, He did not create us because He was lonely! If that were the case, it would have been simple for God to create robots, which would be programmed to display love for Him at every moment. Instead, He gave us life, free will and the ability to love. How much more meaningful it is to receive love when it is given by choice. Imagine a dictator who required absolute obedience and love. People might obey him, and very likely would display the outward signs of love, but that love also would be a façade. That kind of love comes from fear. The Gospel-writer and apostle, John, wrote this:

> There is no fear in love; but perfect love casts out fear, because fear involves torment. But he who fears has not been made perfect in love.
> 1 John 4:18 (NKJV)

Out of self-preservation, we might obey a dictator, and some people incorrectly place God in that same category. Yet God not only created us for love, but He has given us the greatest example of that love, as well. The Bible is God's love letter to man, and while it is a lengthy letter, every word in some manner points to Jesus and what He accomplished on behalf of us all. John shared these words from Jesus:

> Greater love has no one than this, than to lay down one's life

12

for his friends.
John 15:13 (NKJV)

Think about that statement for a moment. Whom would you be willing to die for? Mothers often can have a deeper bond with their children, and we could base that on the biological fact that carrying a life within them for nine months increases that bond. Yet we cannot draw the conclusion that all mothers love this way, either. Certainly, there are fathers who love their children just as deeply. This statement from Jesus specifically mentions friends, though. What friends are you willing to die for? If life is the most precious gift, then to be willing to give that life up to save the life of another demonstrates an amazing depth of love. Before departing for the United States Air Force Academy many years ago, I remember a conversation I had with my mother. I told her that I wanted to become a hero. She wasn't highly educated, but could have had a Master's degree in common sense. She stated, "The only real heroes are dead heroes."

At that time in my life, I was more interested in accomplishing something great and being remembered for it than living a long, happy life. To be remembered comes with the fact that you are not with those remembering you, as we do not have to remember a face we are staring at, do we? We might choose to remember a hero who died for others, but that person's life has reached its end. There were many heroes on 9-11, just as there were on D-Day or Pearl Harbor Day. And as much as the people of the United States might glorify its own heroes of those days, in the Arab, German and Japanese worlds, a different set of heroes may be remembered, though fighting for different results. Jesus' statement should give all of us points to ponder. Are there friends we love so deeply that we would sacrifice our own lives?

Paul takes this to a whole, new level in Romans:

> But God demonstrates His own love toward us, in that while we were still sinners, Christ died for us.
> Romans 5:8 (NKJV)

13

Certainly, Jesus must have called me His friend long before I was willing to call Him my friend, but at that time, He loved me so much that He chose to die for me! While I was still a sinner, with animosity for the God who made the rules I wanted to break, Jesus was willing to give His life for mine. That is quite different than dying for a friend. Instead, Jesus loved His enemies so much that He was willing to die for them, as well. It was not just His death that was heroic, but every aspect of His eternal existence. Jesus existed eternally, before the world began, and He chose to depart heaven. This departure was not for His own glory and honor. Instead, Jesus came for us to ridicule Him, mock Him, wrongly accuse Him, and brutally kill Him. A poet once wrote, "He died upon a cross of wood, yet made the hill on which it stood." The Creator of the universe actually died on the earth He created and was killed by people He created. We all realize our own mortality, but would we ever consider the possibility of God dying, or even more importantly, God dying for us? Others continued to taunt Jesus at the cross, saying that if He really were the God that He claimed to be, Jesus could come down from that cross on His own. Though meant as a taunt, His detractors spoke truth, at least with that statement. I wish I had come up with this phrase on my own, but regardless of its author, it means so much: "It wasn't the nails that held Him to the tree; it was His love for you and me!" Those were my taunts at the cross every bit as much as the taunts of others, yet Jesus still loved me.

Jesus came to give His life for us. I believe that His love is unique, as well. For example, if all of the rest of the world were His followers, and I was alone walking in sin, Jesus loves me so much that He would have come to die for me alone. That is how much He loves each of us. Forget the love songs of hyperbole on the radio. Would you really climb the highest mountain or swim the deepest sea to demonstrate your love to another? If your answer was anything less than a complete denial, you would be lying. We won't even leave the toilet seat down (or up) for another, or make sure the cap is on the toothpaste. But Jesus would do anything. In fact, He already did! If we choose not to receive His love, that is up to us, not Him.

As believers, He calls us to love God and love others. That's not much of a challenge if all it requires is for us to love those who love us. The real challenge for us is to love those who are not so easy to love. How do you feel about the homeless man down the street? How about the drug dealer in the house next door? If we need an example, all we need to do is to look upon the cross! This book is not a romance novel, but it is about love, likely a different kind of love than you ever have imagined. Personally, I do not believe we can begin to love others until we have received God's love and also understood God's love. Once that love becomes a part of us, and we learn how to love others in the same manner God loves us, lives change. That kind of love will not just change us, but can change everyone we come in contact with.

In my other books, I painstakingly have tried to remove myself from the books, though people who know me claim they could hear me speaking while they were reading. My attempt was to have it not sound "preachy." As a sinner saved by grace, I did not want others to think I was talking down to them. Therefore, I wrote in third person, and rarely, if ever, shared personal stories or revelations. But for this book, I made an attempt to bring myself into the book. I still do not want it to sound "preachy." Quite the contrary, as I feel like I supplanted Paul as the "chief of sinners." Every day, I am amazed that God was willing and able to forgive my sin, and loved me enough to call me His own. I do not have the right to preach down to anyone, but what I can do is share the wisdom God has imparted to me. I am talking to you, not talking down to you! I decided to put myself in the story because the story is mine, well, God's and mine, for this has been my journey with Him!

This book is separated into three parts. In the first part, we will put some work into understanding God's love, while in the second part, the focus will be upon receiving God's love. We do not need to know everything about God's love before we can receive it, but before we get behind the wheel of a powerful car, we should know that it is not a tricycle. Finally, God tells us what to do with that love, to offer it to others, and we will discuss that in the third part. May God's love enrich your life as much as it has enriched mine!

Part One, Understanding God's Love

Chapter One:
The Journey Begins

All of our journeys are unique. As believers, our walks with God are
also unique. Just think of the depth described in the word "walk."
It involves slow, progressive movement, sometimes meandering. It
also includes intimacy, when that walk involves another, with time
and closeness to discuss the most personal details of our lives. That
closeness typically becomes closer if the walks occur frequently.
This book details some of the lessons learned on my personal
journey with the Lord. That does not mean it is so unique and so
different from your walks that some of the information included
will not be beneficial. In fact, most of the lessons included are life
lessons, with no greater goal than simplifying the journey of another
and enriching the lives of others. If you were walking a 20-mile
stretch with only one watering hole, and the water was not visible
from the road, most people would want to know the hole's location
to ensure they did not miss it. And yes, there are those people who
would rather find the water on their own. Like a man who refuses to
ask for directions, there is still a time and place for both.

Certainly, this journey began for me the day I asked Jesus to be the Lord and Savior of my life. Frankly, it could have started before that, as God has a purpose and plan in each of our lives, and certainly knew each wrong turn and pitfall I would choose. He used those earlier events to teach me lessons years down the road, too. Since becoming a believer, while both teaching Bible studies and attending Bible studies led by others, I often have heard God and the attributes of God completely misrepresented. I have come to the realization that misunderstanding God's attributes is fairly common in Christianity. Part of this could have to do with incorrect teaching, but just as easily, it also could have to do with our own pride or laziness. After all, God wrote His love letter to each of us, and learning about Him involves digging into the Bible. Yet many would rather listen to a 30-minute sermon than read the Bible, even though when we read the Bible on our own, we can receive that teaching directly from God! Some people learn lessons more easily, but some of the most valuable lessons are the ones that did not come easily. I do not claim to understand everything, either. But this book comes from my heart, to impart some of that heart knowledge I have received to others on the same journey. It is not outlandish that God would be willing to teach His own children! After all, before Jesus departed earth, He told us about the Holy Spirit, whom He would leave in His place:

> But the Helper, the Holy Spirit, whom the Father will send in My name, He will teach you all things, and bring to your remembrance all things that I said to you.
> John 14:26 (NKJV)

All things? Wouldn't that make us all "know-it-alls?" We are God's children, and He wants us to learn about Him, and learn His ways. Jesus lived as an example to us all, and God wants us to simply emulate Him. Without a doubt, God places us in situations to learn, and if we do not learn when in the midst of a trial, chances are highly likely we will find ourselves in a very similar trial over and over again until we learn the desired lesson. Many people pray for trials to be removed, but without trials, we would neither learn nor grow. A better prayer would be that we learn the lesson that God desires on our first time through!

In one Bible study, I was teaching a group of men about the Vine in John 15. In addition to teaching the verses, I was trying to teach them how to interpret the verses correctly themselves, by using inductive Bible study tools. Basically, that process begins by observing the passage, and asking many journalistic questions, though without answering the questions. In the next step, interpretation, we try to answer those questions, and often, the answers are more easily understood by using other Bible verses with some of the same key words. After all, the best interpreter of the Bible is the Bible. Similar to an archaeologist digging for dinosaur bones, the more time we spend observing – brushing the dirt away to expose the buried bones – the less time it will take during interpretation – digging up the bones. If we don't correctly observe the passage, then finding the correct interpretation will become more challenging, if not impossible. Finally, an inductive Bible study finishes with application, personally applying those verses to our own lives. Certainly, application is the most important step. While there is only one correct interpretation, there can be many correct applications. While teaching John 15, I put these verses up on the screen, and asked the men what was the most important word in the passage:

[1] "I am the true vine, and My Father is the vinedresser. [2] Every branch in Me that does not bear fruit He takes away; and every *branch* that bears fruit He prunes, that it may bear more fruit. [3] You are already clean because of the word which I have spoken to you. [4] Abide in Me, and I in you. As the branch cannot bear fruit of itself, unless it abides in the vine, neither can you, unless you abide in Me.
[5] "I am the vine, you *are* the branches. He who abides in Me, and I in him, bears much fruit; for without Me you can do nothing. [6] If anyone does not abide in Me, he is cast out as a branch and is withered; and they gather them and throw *them* into the fire, and they are burned. [7] If you abide in Me, and My words abide in you, you will ask what you desire, and it shall be done for you. [8] By this My Father is glorified, that you bear much fruit; so you will be My disciples.
[9] "As the Father loved Me, I also have loved you; abide in My

love. [10] If you keep My commandments, you will abide in My love, just as I have kept My Father's commandments and abide in His love. [11] "These things I have spoken to you, that My joy may remain in you, and *that* your joy may be full. John 15:1-11 (NKJV)

Interestingly, more than half of the men in the group thought that the most important word of the passage was "prunes." Anyone but a dried grape should be offended. Really? Prunes?! I pointed out to them that in the New King James Version, in only 11 verses, John used the word "love" five times. Not to be outdone, we also see the word "abide" used 10 times. "Branch" occurs four times; "fruit" and "bear" are used together six times; "joy" is used twice; and finally, we see the word "prunes" used once. What would make that word jump off the page to so many people? In my estimation, there is not a more important passage to understand anywhere in the Bible than this one. In John 15:12, in the verse following this passage, Jesus discusses the details of our relationship to others, to love others just as He loves us. How interesting that first, we must learn how to abide in the Vine, as a branch. Branches do not work hard to produce fruit, but receive all needed nourishment from the Vine. We also cannot discount the part in the process that the Vinedresser plays, keeping the branches healthy. In the analogy used by Jesus, the Vinedresser is the Father and Jesus is the Vine, and we as believers are the branches, Christians who desperately need both the Father and Son! I will discuss more about the Vine in the third chapter, but for now, let's go back to my original question.

Why was the word "prunes" singled out by more than half of the seemingly mature, Christian believers in the room? To most, "prunes" speaks of God's punishment when we do not obey His commandments. In fact, a Christian author sold millions of books drawing this erroneous conclusion. The Greek word for "prunes" used in this passage is *katheiro* (καθαίρω). Specifically, that word means "to cleanse," but even in the agricultural usage of the word "prunes," that process involves cutting back branches to help them grow more healthily and fruitfully. Frankly, I doubt a branch ever screamed when a gardener pruned it, but we somehow see this word, equate it with pain, and immediately run in fear. Part of that might have to do with punitive parents, and it is easy to see where a man who never could please his father as a child would come to that assessment. In fact, the ringleader of the group stating that "prunes" was the most important word in the passage came from exactly that kind of upbringing, and sadly, passed those same judgments upon anyone around him that he thought had "missed the mark." Another often misinterpreted word in the John 15 passage is in that same, second verse, stating that each branch that does not bear fruit, He (the Vinedresser) "takes away." The Greek word translated as "takes away" in this passage is *airo* (αἴρω), which is another questionable interpretation. Most of the other times this Greek word is used in the Bible, it is translated as "lifts up." Here is an example:

> Now when these things begin to happen, look up and lift up your heads, because your redemption draws near."
> Luke 21:28 (NKJV)

(Also see John 4:35). This kind of "lifting up" is not to be confused with being exalted. That is a different Greek word, *hupsoo* (ὑψόω). Think of the role of a Vinedresser, who enters His vineyard and sees a branch down in the dirt. Does He yank it from the Vine and take it away, or does He caringly lift that branch out of the dirt, brushing the dirt off and give it a healthier place to grow? All we have to do is to visit a vineyard to see the answer. Even when we fail, and fall into the dirt of sin, our Father picks us up, dusts us off and loves us! None of our sin surprises Him, as God knows everything. It occurred to me that God never has said, "It occurred to Me!"

My approach with this group of men was an immediate assignment. I asked them to spend the week thinking about the harshest punishment God had given them in their years as believers, and then at our next meeting, I wanted each man to share his story. One man came up to me and asked if he thought we would all have a chance to share on one night. Think about your own lives before moving ahead now, and it is likely your lives will parallel ours. The next week, it took seven minutes for all of us to relate our personal stories. Not one man came up with an example of a harsh punishment inflicted on them by the Lord. This does not mean that God does not punish His children. In fact, there are many verses telling us about that punishment. Here is an example from Hebrews:

> [5] And you have forgotten the exhortation which speaks to you as to sons:
> *"My son, do not despise the chastening of the Lord,*
> *Nor be discouraged when you are rebuked by Him;*
> [6] *For whom the Lord loves He chastens,*
> *And scourges every son whom He receives."*
> [7] If you endure chastening, God deals with you as with sons; for what son is there whom a father does not chasten?
> Hebrews 12:5-7 (NKJV)

We also need to be cautious when attributing hardship in our lives to God, and not instead owning that our decisions caused the hardship. Additionally, hardship can be an attack from Satan. This is prevalent in the Book of Job. In that book, Job experienced much hardship, and unfortunately, his three closest friends believed that it all had to do with God's punishment. Eliphaz told Job,

> "Behold, happy is the man whom God corrects;
> Therefore do not despise the chastening of the Almighty.
> Job 5:17 (NKJV)

Eliphaz' statement is correct, as we should be happy when God "chastens" us. That demonstrates how much He loves us and that all He wants for us is for sin to no longer be such a weighty burden. But studying the Book of Job, we also could see that what Job endured had nothing to do with his previous sins. With Job's wife prodding her husband to "curse God and die," and Job's three dearest friends refusing to believe him, Job's self–righteousness grew. Previously, in a conversation with Satan, God had identified Job as His most righteous servant on the earth, and in this process, God allowed Satan to attack Job to prove a point. Additionally, God's plan, brought to fruition, was to draw His closest servant even closer! The Greek word used for "chastening," often translated as "punishment" in many versions of the Bible, is *paideuo* (παιδεύω).

24

Literally, this word means "the training of children." Take a moment to reflect on the punishment you received as a child, and if you are parents, also think of the punishment you have given to your children.

Loving parents are not heavy handed. Most of us have heard the phrase, "this is going to hurt me a lot more than it hurts you." I always wanted to say, "Yeah, right!" and think I probably did a few times. Certainly, there is a wide spectrum of parenting and discipline. Some children may have received severe beatings for the most innocuous offenses, like if they were five minutes late arriving at the dinner table. Other parents, in an attempt to not offend their child, have great difficulty even mentioning bad behavior. God, as our Father, doesn't fit in either category, as He is the perfect Father. He knows exactly what will benefit us and help us grow. We could wrongly assess, "Let the punishment fit the crime," but before going there, we might want to reflect on God's inability to overlook sin. Remember, one sin makes each of us sinners, and the penalty of one sin is no different than the penalty of a million sins – death. But Jesus already paid the price for our sin, so God will not punish us with death if we have asked Jesus to be our Lord and Savior. That would be double jeopardy. But God still desires for us to learn and grow. That involves walking away from sins that are weighing us down. God does this through encouragement.

Many have earthly examples of fathers who teach in this manner, and many Christian fathers teach their children with love as the driving force, as well. This is a much better picture of how God punishes us than a trip to the woodshed! Many of us might think we deserve a trip to the woodshed, but we are to love others the same way God loves us, by edifying others. He wants us to build up others, not tear them down, and in the same manner, God edifies His children rather than tearing them down. Early in my Christian walk, after reading this verse that God chastens His children because He loves them, when I did not experience the immediate, harsh punishment that I thought my sin called for, I was saddened, thinking that I must not be a child of God. But as I grew, I realized that God's punishment was perfect, and different from the punishment given out by imperfect people. I remember one such event from my childhood most vividly. My father had purchased some brownies for a special occasion and placed them out of reach of the children, on top of the refrigerator. The next day, the brownies were gone. My older sister had eaten them, and told my parents that she saw me eating the brownies. I angrily denied it, at the same time that she angelically recounted seeing me eating the brownies. They believed her, and my punishment was harsh, at least in my opinion. In addition to a spanking, I had to spend two weeks in my room, every moment that I was not in school, other than a brief trip to the table for a meal. Again, imperfect people punish imperfectly. In this case, they did not have the right criminal. Even at that age, my self-righteousness fueled my anger. Possibly the larger effect, though, was that my parents were no longer on a pedestal in my childlike trust of them. I thought they knew everything, but realized they did not have a clue. That punishment became a chip on my shoulder. Imagine if Jesus felt the same way about us! After all, He took our punishment, but He did it willingly. Even if I took one on the chin for something I did not do, there were plenty of other times when I avoided a deserved punishment. God's punishment is always couched in love and edification, and not harsh or undeserved.

Sadly, many strong believers still think of God as a punishing God. The Bible reminds us that He is slow to anger, so do not assign similar behavior to God that we exhibit. This may include a harsh word because we are having a bad day, jumping to the wrong conclusion, or being embarrassed by our children's behavior, pridefully, believing it points to our own failures in parenting. God does not have bad days. He always understands each and every nuance of a situation, including our intent. God is humble, and does not worry about how things might appear to others. We are His children! He does not sleep! Neither does He take His eyes away from us, because He loves us.

This year in particular, I have done a lot of thinking about my sister Julee, who is suffering tremendously with Lyme's disease. She also loves Jesus. I have reminded her that God is incapable of giving bad gifts to His children. Certainly, God is using this to bring her closer to Him. As a mother, she loves her son so much. It is difficult to believe anyone could love more than she loves, but we all would be sadly mistaken, comparing our love to the love of God. Jesus reminded us:

> [7] "Ask, and it will be given to you; seek, and you will find; knock, and it will be opened to you. [8] For everyone who asks receives, and he who seeks finds, and to him who knocks it will be opened. [9] Or what man is there among you who, if his son asks for bread, will give him a stone? [10] Or if he asks for a fish, will he give him a serpent? [11] If you then, being evil, know how to give good gifts to your children, how much more will your Father who is in heaven give good things to those who ask Him!
> Matthew 7:7-11 (NKJV)

God loves my sister much more than my sister loves her son, and as she never would give her son a bad gift, why would God give His children bad gifts? God does not just love us; God is love! God does not relish in my sister's suffering, any more than He relished in Job's suffering. But at the same time, God does not make mistakes. If He allows something to happen, He still has a purpose and a plan. Even though we may never know the specific reasons, we always can come to the conclusion that God desires for us to draw closer to Him. That is His purpose in everything! We also should tread lightly when dealing with a friend or family member enduring trials or adversity. "I know exactly what you are feeling," is not only the wrong thing to say, but completely inaccurate. All of us are different, and each situation is different. If Job's friends had not uttered a word, but would have just sat beside him and cried with him, Job would not have felt the need to defend himself. We all just need love! Remembering the biggest failure of Job's friends might also remind us not to equate someone's suffering with God's punishment. We do not have the right to speak for God, and certainly, cannot read His mind. As teachers, we must be cautious not to misrepresent God. It is one thing to lead yourself down the wrong path, and quite another to lead others into danger.

Another passage from a Bible study also caused me to think deeply about God's love. The teacher lectured on Romans 12, and then we got to this section:

> [18] If it is possible, as much as depends on you, live peaceably with all men. [19] Beloved, do not avenge yourselves, but rather give place to wrath; for it is written, *"Vengeance is Mine, I will repay,"* says the Lord. [20] Therefore
> *"If your enemy is hungry, feed him;*
> *If he is thirsty, give him a drink;*
> *For in so doing you will heap coals of fire on his head."*
> [21] Do not be overcome by evil, but overcome evil with good.
> Romans 12:18-21 (NKJV)

In this passage, Paul quotes Proverbs 25:21-22, giving believers instructions on the desired relationship God has for us with combative unbelievers. Our response should not be negatively affected by their response. Regardless of how they treat us, we are to be kind to our enemies. That kindness includes being concerned with their sustenance and survival, as we are to feed them if hungry and provide drink if they are thirsty. We also see their probable response, which is one we might not expect. It sure sounds to me like they will become increasingly hostile, or at least completely confused why someone they hate so much could be so kind to them. What we do not see in either the Old Testament or New Testament passages is that kindness of this manner will cause our enemies to rethink their hate and/or anger for us, and treat us better. We can overcome evil with good. But the Bible teacher sharing this passage equated it with hell, drawing a correlation between the hot coals and the fire and brimstone of hell. Yet scripturally, that interpretation makes no sense. Why would God remind us of hell at the same time He is encouraging us to love our enemies? Are we to take joy that one day, God will have vengeance upon those who mistreated us? Instead, shouldn't we be heartbroken that people will perish?

There is an interesting video on YouTube where Penn Jillette, a noted atheist, comedian, actor and magician, relates a story about a Christian, who remained after a show to give him a Bible. Though

28

Jillette's beliefs could not be more different from that Christian's, Jillette made an interesting comment. He summarized his logic, that if we truly believe that people who do not put their faith in Jesus will burn for eternity in hell, how much do we have to hate them to NOT tell them about Jesus? Jillette said, "I don't respect people who don't proselytize." Our hearts should break for unbelievers, not gloat about their future demise.

I heard another story of a Christian woman, whose husband was a mean drunk. He often would come home in the wee hours of the night, with equally drunken friends in tow, wake his wife and order her to cook breakfast for her husband and his friends. One of those friends watched her closely. She did not complain, and lovingly prepared the meal for them all. That friend asked her how she could treat her husband so well when he was so mean to her, and she said, "When I leave this earth, I will spend eternity with my Lord and Savior, Jesus Christ. For my husband, though, earth is the closest thing to heaven he ever will experience. I will do my best to show God's love to him here, and maybe, he will see how Jesus loves him!"

If we understand God's heart for the lost and emulate that kind of love, we will share God's love with everyone we come in contact with. The action of loving others is more powerful than mere words. God's Word does not conflict itself, stating one thing in one verse and the opposite in another verse. We are His creation. He wants us all to be saved.

> [3] For this *is* good and acceptable in the sight of God our Savior, [4] who desires all men to be saved and to come to the knowledge of the truth. [5] For *there is* one God and one Mediator between God and men, *the* Man Christ Jesus, [6] who gave Himself a ransom for all, to be testified in due time,
> 1 Timothy 2:3-6 (NKJV)

This made me think of the story of Jonah. God had a plan for Jonah, and it involved Nineveh. But Jonah despised the Ninevites. They were his enemies, and even though Jonah was a man of God, the last thing he wanted to do was to take salvation to such an evil city. Jonah got on a slow boat to Tarshish rather than a slow boat to China, but God changed the destination by taking Jonah from the boat and having him personally escorted in the belly of a giant fish. Still, Jonah fought with God about delivering a message of repentance and salvation to the people of Nineveh. Jonah must have known that the entire city would repent and turn to the Lord, and he did not want to share heaven with them. Regardless of the failures of Jonah, God prevailed. Every Ninevite repented and turned to the Lord! Who are the Ninevites in your life?

Recently, I drove to Williamstown, Kentucky to see Ark Encounter. Through the efforts of Ken Ham, an ark has been built with the biblical proportions of 300 cubits in length, 50 cubits in width and 30 cubits in height. A cubit is the distance from the bottom of the bend in a man's elbow to the tip of his middle finger. Ham based his ark on a 20-inch cubit, and the result is mind-blowing. The ark is 500 feet in length, 83 feet wide and 50 feet high. Picture a 100-yard long football field and then understand this ark is 166 yards long! I walked around the outside of the ark for a couple hours, praising the Lord, taking photos and thinking. Noah spent 100 years building his ark. That points to a plan, and we know that the plan came from God. In those 100 years, Noah told everyone he could about the upcoming flood, and when my eyes saw this immense structure, I thought that even with all the animals aboard, there still would have been lots of room for many people. The ark was an Old Testament model of salvation, pointing forward to the work Jesus would accomplish on the cross. The ark had one door; and Jesus is the door, the only way, the only truth and the only life! Just as the ark carried the family of Noah, eight people in total, to a new life, Jesus offers us that new life, too. That was the same message that day as I looked upon this re-creation of the ark. Just as Paul wrote in his letter to Timothy, God's heart is that everyone would be saved. Why would a God with redemption on His mind desire for us to take joy in another man's punishment of hell?

Again, that misinterpretation of the passage in Romans presents God in a punitive, rather than loving way. Sometimes, we have difficulty understanding this balance. For example, think of the judgments of Revelation, where God prophetically speaks of a coming time when He will pour out His wrath on a sinful earth. Does God's wrath conflict His love? On the contrary, even when wrathful, God is 100% loving. That might be difficult for our finite brains to comprehend, but just understand that God's desire is that all men would be saved. Our logic should at least follow that as He created each of us, He loves us. A common adage is that there are no atheists in foxholes, as when under extreme duress, people who have not considered their own mortality will do so. Certainly, the judgments of Revelation will cause many to look to a God they chose not to honor with their lives. Many will still choose not to believe, but God's heart is that everyone would be saved, and He has gone to the extreme to show us this!

Remember though, God is the judge, not us. For man to call down God's judgment on an earthly enemy points to man's failure, not God's. In Psalm 69, King David poured out his heart to God for help, when under attack from his enemies. Here is a section of that:

> [21] They also gave me gall for my food,
> And for my thirst they gave me vinegar to drink.
> [22] Let their table become a snare before them,
> And their well-being a trap.
> [23] Let their eyes be darkened, so that they do not see;
> And make their loins shake continually.
> [24] Pour out Your indignation upon them,
> And let Your wrathful anger take hold of them.
> [25] Let their dwelling place be desolate;
> Let no one live in their tents.
> [26] For they persecute the *ones* You have struck,
> And talk of the grief of those You have wounded.
> [27] Add iniquity to their iniquity,
> And let them not come into Your righteousness.
> [28] Let them be blotted out of the book of the living,
> And not be written with the righteous.
> Psalm 69:21-28 (NKJV)

For context, it would be worth reading this entire psalm, but here, we see David in a frustrated state. David questioned, as do all of us at times, why evil people seem to prosper. The simplest of answers is that we are putting far too much emphasis on this earth. A time will come very soon when all God's enemies will be vanquished, but now is not that time. Instead, God gives every man the opportunity to find Him, and that discovery can take us through the messiest sin, the most hateful actions and the saddest failures. Before Paul became a believer on the Damascus Road, imagine these prayers to the Lord from believers of the time whom Paul was persecuting. It would be ignorant of me to think I was not that same burden on another Christian before I came to know Jesus. Yet we need to hear David's frustration, empathize with him, and also know that God is calling us to react in a different way. When we think of what Jesus endured on the cross, we know that nothing could have been worse. Matthew writes,

> And about the ninth hour Jesus cried out with a loud voice, saying, "Eli, Eli, lama sabachthani?" that is, *"My God, My God, why have You forsaken Me?"*
> Matthew 27:46 (NKJV)

In this statement by Jesus, He restated a prophetic verse from Psalm 22, and revealed the greatest pain in history. Throughout the New Testament, Jesus referred to His Father, and then in this passage, we see that loss of relationship, in the words "My God, My God," instead of "My Father." Personally, I think that by saying "My God" twice, Jesus was speaking to God the Father and to the Holy Spirit. When our sins were placed on the shoulders of Jesus, as God could not look upon sin, the Father turned His head, and Jesus experienced a momentary loss of relationship with the Father, and His relationship with the Holy Spirit was also temporarily absent. At the same time, the Father's relationship with Jesus was also absent. That was anguish. Imagine the anguish that others will feel at Judgment Day when confronted with the God they chose not to believe in. After seeing God's righteousness, they will be separated from that All-Mighty God for all of eternity. Jesus' anguish lasted for moments, but compare that to the eternal anguish that those who choose not to honor God while on this earth will experience. If we know the anguish that will occur in the lives of those who do not believe, why would we ever want additional torment for those people?

Instead, we should leave vengeance to the Lord, and pour our love onto others. Wasn't it God's love that drew us to the Lord? I have spent so much time reflecting upon this. God is completely righteous, but I was not drawn to His righteousness. In fact, when I experience His righteousness and rightly assess my own unrighteousness, I feel completely unworthy, and unable to envision myself in His presence. God's righteousness makes me feel separated from Him. But I am drawn to God by His love and grace, for through that love and grace, He built a bridge to bring me from my unrighteousness to His righteousness. That bridge was the cross. Without the life and sacrificial death of Jesus, my own sins would have required punishment by my own death.

Before proceeding, understand a stark difference between a believer and an unbeliever. As just mentioned, a believer is a child of God, and because of that, his sins already have been punished. Better than the movie, "Trading Places," Jesus traded places with us. Though He never had sinned, Jesus took our places on the cross, and received God's death and judgment for our sins. And at the same time, we take His place, standing before God, clothed in the righteousness that Jesus earned with His perfect life. That is exactly what this verse is saying:

> For He made Him who knew no sin *to be* sin for us, that we might become the righteousness of God in Him.
> 2 Corinthians 5:21 (NKJV)

God the Father made the sinless Jesus to bear our sin, and adorned us with Christ's righteousness. As believers, when God looks at us, He sees Jesus, and additionally, when Jesus was on the cross, God saw our sin and looked away. This might not make sense to us, as we have difficulty understanding the stark difference between righteousness and unrighteousness. In the Bible, anyone in the presence of God felt so unworthy that they were face down in the dirt. When John was taken up to heaven to see the future events he would describe in Revelation, John even felt unworthy in the presence of an angel, and when bowing, the angel corrected John that he only should bow to God, not another created being. John was the "disciple Jesus loved," but when in the presence of the glorified Jesus, John rightly felt the same separation of unworthiness between the righteous Jesus and unrighteous man. The simple miracle of this all is that as believers, God sees us as righteous. Adopted into His family, He knows we are not perfect children, but He is the perfect Father. As that perfect Father, every action is to build us, to make us more like Him in how we think, how we act, and especially, how we love!

Contrastingly, how does God look at an unbeliever? With disdain? Do not forget, He created them, too. With certainty, God knows every person that ever will walk this earth that will choose to be His child. But even for those who never will know Him while on this earth, God still is faithful and gives them every opportunity. As every human to live is God's creation, also do not misunderstand and think we are all children of God. To be His child requires His adoption, and our desire to be called by His name. At the Day of Judgment, when those who chose not to believe in the God who offered to save them stand in front of God, three events will occur. First, when confronted with the God they chose not to believe in, there will be no more argument.

> [5] Let this mind be in you which was also in Christ Jesus, [6] who, being in the form of God, did not consider it robbery to be equal with God, [7] but made Himself of no reputation, taking the form of a bondservant, *and* coming in the likeness of men. [8] And being found in appearance as a man, He humbled Himself and became obedient to *the point of* death, even the death of the cross. [9] Therefore God also has highly exalted Him and given Him the name which is above every name, [10] that at the name of Jesus every knee should bow, of those in heaven, and of those on earth, and of those under the earth, [11] and *that* every tongue should confess that Jesus

Christ *is* Lord, to the glory of God the Father.
Philippians 2:5-11 (NKJV)

Every knee shall bow and also, every tongue will confess! Now, on earth, a separation exists between believers and unbelievers, but after God's Judgment, all will be believers. That may be difficult to understand, but at that time, all will acknowledge Jesus as Lord. But it will be too late for those who refused Jesus while they were on this earth. At the Judgment, those who chose not to believe while on earth will be punished with hell. For all of eternity. That will be much worse than any trip to the woodshed! Some of the sins of my life still make me feel so much shame. We see in the Bible that God separates our sin as far as the east is from the west; He casts our sin into the depths of the ocean; and God puts our sin behind His back. Imagine! The God who knows all chooses to forget our sin. But He still allows us to remember that sin. Why? Does He want us to feel shame? I think He wants us to have compassion for others struggling in sin, remembering where we walked before He saved us. Instead of looking upon an unbeliever as a loser, we should see ourselves before we knew Jesus, in them. Everyone is redeemable! As believers, we should not be fearful of punishment, only concerned with blessings. For God's punishment is a blessing to a believer. God is incapable of giving a bad gift to His children, so any chastening would still have to be a blessing. That is one of the rights of adoption into the family of God!

But we still try to attribute our difficulties to God's punishment. Maybe we would do better to attribute those difficulties to our own choices. One Gospel story brings this most alive to me. All of us know of the events leading up to the crucifixion. Peter, a big-hearted and courageous man, bragged to Jesus that he loved Jesus more than the rest. Jesus knew exactly what was about to happen, and He told Peter.

> Jesus said to him, "Assuredly, I say to you that this night, before the rooster crows, you will deny Me three times."
> Matthew 26:34 (NKJV)

35

Jesus was not "piling on," and at least in my mind's eye, I hear that verse with immense sadness. Of course, it happened exactly as Jesus said it would. Those events included the arrest of Jesus in the Garden of Gethsemane, where Peter pulled out a sword and sliced off the ear of Malchus, one of the guards. Jesus healed the ear of Malchus. Why? Without that healing, Peter would have been arrested, and likely, put to death. But Jesus had more work for Peter to accomplish. That included Peter writing two books of the New Testament, in addition to the Gospel of Mark, often attributed to Peter as John Mark was Peter's secretary of sorts. The Gospel of Mark is very likely the Perspective of Peter!

What did Jesus do after the resurrection? One of His first stops was to restore Peter. We will discuss that more deeply in chapter two, but think about this. Can you imagine a more egregious sin than denying Jesus? Peter denied knowing Jesus multiple times, on the night when we would think Jesus needed Peter the most. We nebulously assign degrees upon our sins. Some even come up with their own official ranking system of venial sins and mortal sins. But whatever sin we commit, and if we were to commit only one, that sin must be punished by death. Is there sin in your life that you believe God cannot forgive? He forgave Peter for denying Jesus! God forgave Moses for murder. God forgave His favorite Israelite king, David, for adultery and murder. Christians are not perfect people. Christians are flawed sinners, who made one right decision to follow the One True God and receive His forgiveness. Though we are separated from God by our sin, He built a bridge. Again, I see that bridge in the form of a wooden cross. What kind of love does that require? Peter was broken, but his own decisions caused that brokenness. Yet Jesus restored Peter, nonetheless.

One of my previous pastors struggled with an addiction to alcohol before becoming a Christian. After he was saved, he said that when he took a sip of beer, it tasted like urine. He never drank again. Years later, a lady in his congregation was struggling with drug addiction.

The pastor told her that if she ever took another drug, she would go to hell. Sadly, he took the miracle that God had performed in his own life and turned it into a doctrine. He turned God into a punitive God, when there was no verse in the Bible to support his statement. There are many sins I have continued to struggle with as a believer, but as I walk with the Lord, I can see some of those struggles disappearing. When I look in the mirror, I do not see the same man that I did 15 years ago, 10 years ago, 5 years ago. It is a process, and God's process is unique and special for each of us.

Let me also emphasize that I am not avoiding the biblical teaching of God's wrath. We see that in the Great Flood, the plagues in Egypt and the parting of the Red Sea, Sodom and Gomorrah, the death of Ananias and Sapphira, and the future judgments of Revelation. But as God is slow to anger, make sure to differentiate between His wrath, His judgment and His chastening!

So, this journey begins with a deeper understanding of God's love. Without at least a rudimentary understanding of His love for us, how could that love possibly change our lives? Buckle your seatbelts. Open your eyes. Drop your preconceptions and bring openness to the table, all based on what God's Word tells us. This journey has some twists and turns in the road ahead.

Chapter Two:
Love is the Answer!

Not surprisingly, it all comes down to love. Yet how can we understand all the nuances of this simple, four-letter word, as it is only simple on the surface? Is love earned or freely given? Does love have more to do with the physical, emotional or spiritual? Does love mean the same to everyone? At least at this point in the journey, it seems there are more questions than answers.

Sometimes, as English speakers, we limit ourselves within the confines of our language. The English language, for example, has only one word for love, while in Greek, there are four. So, when speaking English, we would use the same word for extremely different circumstances, while in Greek, usage of a more specific word would help the listener to understand perfectly. Let's take the word "polish," for example. If I told you that we were going to the baseball game and would enjoy a Polish-sausage, would you be surprised if it did not taste like Lemon Pledge? Or if I asked you to "wind the clock," would you surmise that if you blew really hard, the clock would continue to run? The Polish man (from Poland) can clean his furniture with polish, and at the same time can wind the clock and watch an eagle soar in the wind. Obviously, these words are spelled the same, but have completely different meanings. Maybe that is one of the reasons that God chose Greek as the language for the New Testament. After all, if it was important to Him to have numerous men write the words of the Bible over thousands of years, and to have believers understand His specific message, then even something as different as language could have an effect. Certainly, God's choice of original language of the Bible was not just a coincidence. If the New Testament had been written in English originally, then we might miss the differences in the word love. Some of those differences are rather subtle, but others, extreme.

Only two of those four Greek words for love are used in the New Testament, however. *Agape* (ἀγαπάω) is used in both noun and verb formats (see Strong's Concordance G25 and G26 for reference) and *phileo* is only used as a verb (see G5368 in Strong's Concordance for reference). The word for "beloved," (*agapetos*) is closely related to *agape*, using the same root word (see G27 in Strong's Concordance for reference). Greek also has two other words for love that do not appear in the Bible. One is *eros*, which is basically sexual love and involves physical attraction, and the other is *storges*, which is a natural obligation, protection or affection. In the days of arranged marriages, a husband's love for his wife would have been an example of *storges*. Another example would be love for a dog, though I am certain that my love for my dog far surpasses obligation or mere affection! It's interesting that marriage is the only place where we can see all four types of love from Greek!

If you are feeling overwhelmed by delving into Greek for a moment, you might repeat the adage, "Sounds like Greek to me." These words sound like Greek because they are! Though it might stretch us a bit to look into the meaning of these words, it is worth it, more than thinking that love always means the same, just because it does in English.

Let's use *phileo* as a starting point. We can see the root in the name of a large city in the United States, Philadelphia, which means, "brotherly love." This kind of love is not bad, but can be improved upon. In fact, in John 5:20, it says, "the Father loves the Son," and *phileo* is the Greek word for love used in that passage. If it is possible and plausible for the Father to *phileo* the Son, then we should not question whether or not *phileo* is "real" love! In Chapter 1, we discussed the failure of Peter's denial of Jesus just before the crucifixion, and also mentioned that one of the first acts of Jesus after His resurrection was to restore Peter. For a deeper understanding of the differences in these two words for love, let's look at the passage demonstrating this restoration of a broken man.

> [15] So when they had finished breakfast, Jesus said to Simon Peter, "Simon, *son* of John, do you love [*agapao*] Me more than these?" He said to Him, "Yes, Lord; You know that I love [*phileo*] You." He said to him, "Tend My lambs."
> [16] He said to him again a second time, "Simon, *son* of John, do you love [*agapao*] Me?" He said to Him, "Yes, Lord; You know that I love [*phileo*] You." He said to him, "Shepherd My sheep."
> [17] He said to him the third time, "Simon, *son* of John, do you love [*phileo*] Me?" Peter was grieved because He said to him the third time, "Do you love [*phileo*] Me?" And he said to Him, "Lord, You know all things; You know that I love [*phileo*] You." Jesus said to him, "Tend My sheep.
> John 21:15-17 (NASB)

Jesus and Peter seem to be speaking a different language, and though this was retold in Greek, they could have been speaking Koine Greek, Aramaic (which was the common spoken language of Jews of that time) or Hebrew, typically used in Jewish religious practices of the time. But the words of the Bible were God-breathed, and consequently, the specifics of this "love language" is God-ordained, not happenstance. It can be a little confusing. When Jesus asked Peter if he *agape* loved him, shouldn't Peter's response have been, "No, I *phileo* love You." But instead, Peter avoided the negative and said, "You know I *phileo* love You." "Is your blood red?" "You know that it is crimson." In the same manner that *agape* and *phileo* are related, red and crimson are, as well. It's not just the Greek words for love in this passage that are more specific than English, either. We also can see specifics in Jesus' three admonishments to Peter of "feed My lambs" (baby lambs), "tend My sheep" (adult sheep), and "feed My sheep" (adult sheep). In this passage, Jesus asked Peter about a different kind of love – *agape*. How does *agape* differ from *phileo*? When I think about love, these verses from 1 John come to mind:

> [7] Beloved, let us love one another, for love is from God; and everyone who loves is born of God and knows God. [8] The one who does not love does not know God, for God is love. [9] By this the love of God was manifested in us, that God has sent His only begotten Son into the world so that we might live through Him. [10] In this is love, not that we loved God, but that He loved us and sent His Son to be the propitiation for our sins. [11] Beloved, if God so loved us, we also ought to love one another.
> 1 John 4:7-11 (NASB)

Let's consider a variety of people walking the earth. As stated earlier, the desire for love is universal. John correctly states that all love comes from one source, and that source is God, and by the way, each time "love" appears in the passage above it is *agape*. God's love for us began before the foundations of the earth, as even before creation, God had a plan. That plan looked into the future and saw every wrong turn that each of us would make. Consequently, God's love for us did not begin or end at our creation. God's plan included a way to deal with our sin. Until we realize the vast separation between God and man that must exist because of even one sin, we cannot begin to grasp our unworthiness. But let's be honest, none of us have committed just one sin. Our lives are riddled with sin. As hard as I try to live righteously, I don't think I have gone a day without sin. That's pretty depressing, until God reminds me that I never will have to go a day without Him!

Time and energy draw relationships closer, and keeping that in mind, think of the relationship between Jesus and the Father. First of all, they are ONE, so the relationship could not be closer. Yet for all of eternity, the love between Father and Son has been perfect, complete and holy. Can any mother or father consider what it would take to sacrifice their own child? If a father needed a son's heart, or the father would die, would any father kill his own son to extend his own life? That might not be the best analogy, for that kind of love would not be selfless, but selfish. God the Father, who could not possibly love the Son any more than He did, asked Jesus to depart from heaven, and die a brutal death at the hands of mockers. Not only that, but the death of Jesus was for the benefit of the mockers. Jesus died for people who hated Him! When our sins were placed upon Jesus, the closest relationship ever to exist was removed. Again, we see this when Jesus stated, "My God, My God, why have You forsaken Me?" All throughout the Gospels, Jesus referred to God as "Father," but when He made that statement on the cross, that relational term was noticeably absent. Wouldn't that be the most painful, most heartbreaking experience possible? How did the death of Jesus make the Father feel? Isaiah explained it succinctly, "It pleased the Father to bruise Jesus." Amazingly, Isaiah penned that prophetic passage 1,000 years before the cross and before crucifixion was invented. How could the Father be pleased? Because the Father knew that the crucifixion of Jesus was the most important part of the plan. Through the death, burial and resurrection of Jesus, every person to live would have a way of salvation. Salvation would offer the forgiveness of sin, the removal of sin, companionship with God in this life and an eternity to spend in fellowship with the Lord! On the day when Jesus died, Satan likely threw a party, thinking he had finally won. But God snatched that victory away and turned Satan's greatest triumph into Satan's greatest defeat, opening the door for all to come to the Lord!

As children, we can likely remember singing, "Jesus loves me," but certainly, I had no concept of what that love entailed. Perhaps one of the easiest ways to understand *agape* love is to read Paul's love chapter from 1 Corinthians.

> ¹ Though I speak with the tongues of men and of angels, but have not love, I have become sounding brass or a clanging cymbal. ² And though I have *the gift of* prophecy, and understand all mysteries and all knowledge, and though I

have all faith, so that I could remove mountains, but have not love, I am nothing. ³ And though I bestow all my goods to feed *the poor*, and though I give my body to be burned, but have not love, it profits me nothing.

⁴ Love suffers long *and* is kind; love does not envy; love does not parade itself, is not puffed up; ⁵ does not behave rudely, does not seek its own, is not provoked, thinks no evil; ⁶ does not rejoice in iniquity, but rejoices in the truth; ⁷ bears all things, believes all things, hopes all things, endures all things. ⁸ Love never fails. But whether *there are* prophecies, they will fail; whether *there are* tongues, they will cease; whether *there is* knowledge, it will vanish away. ⁹ For we know in part and we prophesy in part. ¹⁰ But when that which is perfect has come, then that which is in part will be done away. ¹¹ When I was a child, I spoke as a child, I understood as a child, I thought as a child; but when I became a man, I put away childish things. ¹² For now we see in a mirror, dimly, but then face to face. Now I know in part, but then I shall know just as I also am known. ¹³ And now abide faith, hope, love, these three; but the greatest of these *is* love.
1 Corinthians 13 (NKJV)

Now, go back and read that again, two more times. The first time through, substitute the name of Jesus for the word love, each time it appears. Then on the final time through, substitute your own name when you see love. The name of Jesus fits just perfectly, but when I place my name into those statements, I see how much work God still has to complete in me. Yet at the same time, it brings clarification to the kind of love that God loves me with, as well as the kind of love God is calling me to share with others. Anytime we forget the depths of God's *agape* love, if we reflect on what Jesus did for us, we can at least get a picture of that unconditional and sacrificial love. Just before His arrest, when Jesus was praying in the Garden of Gethsemane, He asked the Father if there was any other way, to allow this cup to pass from Him. We can learn so much from that prayer alone. As Jesus always prayed in the Father's will, ALL of His prayers were answered! (Our prayers as believers have three answers

– yes, no and not now). For God to still allow the cross tells us that there was no other way. Yet in that prayer, we also can see the heaviness of the burden that Jesus was carrying. With the willingness of Jesus to proceed to the cross, knowing the weight of the burden, we also can know that without love, it could not be possible. Without God, *agape* love is not possible. There is no greater example of God's love, *agape* love, than the cross!

The passage mentioned earlier from 1 John addresses believers, not unbelievers. We can see that in the first word – Beloved! "Beloved" refers to a person dearly loved and cherished greatly. A level of partiality also goes hand-in-hand with this term, as the "beloved" is someone loved more than the others. Again, in the New Testament usage of this term, "beloved" includes the *agape* root, and certainly, that same, *agape* love. Interestingly, John is often referred to in the Bible as "the disciple whom Jesus loved (*agape*). Certainly, Jesus loved (*agape*) all of His disciples, but there was a special love for John. Obviously, "beloved" is a different word in Hebrew, but denotes a similar relationship. "Beloved" is most common in the Song of Solomon, used 32 times in that book alone. In that Old Testament book, we can see the intimacy of the relationship that existed between the beloved.

> My beloved is mine, and I am his;
> He pastures *his flock* among the lilies.
> Song of Solomon 2:16 (NASB)

As Christians, we are the "brides of Christ" and when Jesus returned to heaven, He went to prepare a place for us. It might be hard for a man to think of himself as a future bride, but the God-given covenant of marriage tells us so much about the desired love that Jesus has for each believer. Our culture really has messed this up. A survey done by the Health Survey of England found that the average man has nine sexual partners in his life, while the average woman has four. In most television shows today, "hooking up" is the norm, rather than being perceived as offensive or against God's Law. While modern-day culture makes this practice easier, sin has remained the same throughout time. Think of Solomon with his 700 wives and 300 concubines. But God designed marriage and marital relations as an example of intimacy. If a man and wife were each other's only partners for life, there would be no comparisons to other partners, and the only point of reference would be one of blessing. Years ago, in a men's prayer group, one man asked for prayer concerning issues with his second marriage. She was a godly woman, but his complaint involved the bedroom. After divorcing his first wife, he had been with numerous prostitutes and acquired an addiction to pornography. One of the biggest parts of the problem was that he had lost the intimacy that God intended, and instead, had focused on the carnal, comparing the actions of his wife to actions of prostitutes. It was a perfect example of a time when our perspective and God's perspective are completely different, as this man wanted us to pray for his wife to change, when it was his heart that needed change. God desires the intimacy of a one-on-one relationship with each of us. We are His beloved, and He wants to be our beloved. This relationship has nothing to do with the carnality of matters, but intimacy is key. We can see this intimate relationship between God and Adam in the Garden of Eden. It brings to mind the chorus of the hymn, "In the Garden."

> He walks with me and He talks with me, and He tells me I am His own.
> And the joy we share as we tarry there, none other has ever known.

Anytime we see the word "Beloved" in the Bible, we should pay closer attention, as the God who loves us individually wants to speak something personal to us. Let me paraphrase that 1 John passage by accentuating this with the usage of *agape*. "Beloved, who is very dear to God, let us love (*agape*) one another. For *agape* love is of God and anyone who loves with that *agape* love is born of God and knows God. He who doesn't love with *agape* love does not know God, for God IS that *agape* love!"

Now, the passage makes much more sense, as before, we might misconstrue that anyone who loves another person is God's child. How about an atheist couple? We might see another kind of love in their lives, but without a relationship with God, no one is capable of either giving or receiving *agape* love, the love spoken of in 1 Corinthians 13. God does not just love us in that manner. As the passage says, God is *agape* love! Think for a moment of our earlier exercise, of placing our own names in the place of the word "love" in 1 Corinthians 13. Did it make you feel uncomfortable? Did your mind begin to think of all the times when your love did not measure up to that kind of love, like mine did? That is a bit of a double-edged sword. First of all, it is discouraging to see the number of times we fail, but at the same time, as we know that God has promised to complete His work in us, we can look forward to a time when we will love exactly as God desires, without failing! But if we look inward and see that we never have loved in a way resembling 1 Corinthians 13, then according to John's verses, we do not know God.

John, Paul, George and Ringo might have penned many love songs, but their songs are about a different kind of love. In the Bible, interestingly, John and Paul are the ones who wrote about *agape* love the most. With *agape* as noun, verb and also as a root (beloved), John used this word 97 times, while Paul used *agape* 128 times. Luke 7 involves one of my favorite examples of this word. Jesus told Peter a story of a man who lent money to two different men. To one, he lent a great some of money and to the other, he lent a much lesser amount. Then the generous lender forgave both debts. Jesus asked Peter which borrower would love (*agape*) the lender more. Peter quickly answered, "Well, the one who had the greater debt forgiven," and Jesus responded, "You have judged rightly."

This story, as most of you are keenly aware, is not about money. It is about our debt, and specifically speaking, our sin debt. The work that Jesus did on the cross was for everyone, but by choice, all do not receive that gift. It always makes me think of Christmas morning. The biggest package with the most ornate wrapping might have my name on it, but unless I open that gift, it is useless, nothing more than window dressing. In order to use the gift that Jesus is offering, we have to receive it, receive Him, as our Lord and Savior. But this story in Luke does not explain Jesus' gift, but our response. In his

47

letter to Timothy (1 Timothy 1:15), Paul declared himself the "chief of sinners." Personally, when I reflect on my life before Jesus became the Lord of my life, I feel like I far surpassed Paul for that ignominious title, yet Paul does not know the sins in my life any more than I know the sins in Paul's life. But Paul and I have something in common. Knowing our sin, and knowing the forgiveness given freely by Jesus, we are those who had the greatest debts forgiven. Consequently, our love is immense! This brings up a whole other can of worms. Is it more beneficial to walk deeply in sin and have Jesus forgive that sin, or to sin less and experience less grace? Paul addressed a similar issue in Romans 5 and 6.

Many Jews became self-righteous, adding to God's Laws and spending so much time and energy attempting to adhere to the Law that they were trying to earn salvation. But we know that salvation is a gift, and we are incapable of earning a gift. It can only be freely given. Gentiles, on the other hand, were so amazed by grace (it is amazing grace, isn't it?), that they fell into the trap of more sin, more grace, believing they could not experience grace without sin, so why try to stop sinning? Paul said this,

> [1] What shall we say then? Shall we continue in sin that grace may abound? [2] Certainly not! How shall we who died to sin live any longer in it? [3] Or do you not know that as many of us as were baptized into Christ Jesus were baptized into His death? [4] Therefore we were buried with Him through baptism into death, that just as Christ was raised from the dead by the glory of the Father, even so we also should walk in newness of life.
> Romans 6:1-4 (NKJV)

All of my sins – past, present and future – have been forgiven because of the work that Jesus accomplished on the cross. I cannot add to that work, or take away from it either. After all, Jesus stated, "It is finished," before He died. But when I sin now, I still try to picture that I am placing another burden on the already burdened shoulders of my Savior. Jesus has made my yoke easy and my burden light, if I choose to let Him shoulder my burden, but if all I do is to place more burdens on His shoulders, how much could I possibly *agape* love Him? Yes, sin is our nature, but as believers, we are no longer slaves to sin, as we were before Christ entered our lives. Now, we are slaves to righteousness. Would I rather be the Christian with an abundance of sins forgiven, or the Christian who has walked closely with Jesus for years? My love might be different, because I feel a heavier burden removed from my shoulders, but the enduring, daily walk by a mature Christian is just as special. Just remember that regardless of the size of the burden that He lifted, without His work, we all would be eternally dead!

Another verse comes to mind that does not include the word *agape*, but demonstrates that kind of love to us. In Hebrews, the author quotes Deuteronomy 31:6 and 31:8, stating,

> Let your conduct *be* without covetousness; *be* content with such things as you have. For He Himself has said, *"I will never leave you nor forsake you."*
> Hebrews 13:5 (NKJV)

What an amazing and loving promise from God to every believer! We never will be alone; never will be in a circumstance where He does not have our backs (and our fronts and sides, too); it's not that God decides not to leave our sides, it's that He is incapable of leaving the sides of the ones He loves.

Talk about "never-failing love!" If there were four men on a hike in the wilderness and a grizzly bear attacked, we wouldn't have to outrun the bear. To save ourselves, we would just need to outrun one of the other hikers. If Jesus was on the hike with us, He would tell us to run and would face the bear alone. Think of the pillar of cloud by day and the pillar of fire by night that protected the Jews in the wilderness for 40 years. Pharaoh's advancing army was much more dangerous than a grizzly bear, yet God stood between the Jews and their enemies, and vanquished those enemies with His might. Most people, even our dearest friends and family, will sometimes leave us absolutely alone to face the enemy, while claiming to love us. But that is not *agape* love. *Agape* love is to be willing to die for another, just as the completely innocent Jesus died for my sins.

Here is an additional verse from Romans that also explains God's love in such a special way:

> And we know that all things work together for good to those who love God, to those who are the called according to *His* purpose.
> Romans 8:28 (NKJV)

God is incapable of giving a less-than-perfect gift to His children. Regardless of our sin or choices, our all-powerful and all-knowing God will cause all to work for our good and His glory. That includes my worst decisions. That does not mean that it is going to be easy, though. Sin has consequences, and often our worst decisions place us in situations where we have to deal with those consequences. Let's say a believer commits a murder. This verse is not stating that he will not be convicted or not have to serve the sentence. Nor does it say that God will punish him with hell for that sin. Very likely, the man will go to jail and God will hold his hand throughout. There have been times in my Christian walk when I have become so depressed for falling into sin again. Satan lies to me and tells me that I am not a follower of Christ if I chose to sin in that manner. But then God speaks the whole truth to me. He reminds me that when He saved me, He knew every sin that I ever would commit, including this one, and He still loves me the same. Understand, we do not earn God's love. It is His gift, and His love is not reward given out for our good behavior. I am His child and He loves me regardless of my sin, regardless of my failure and regardless of my good behavior, as well. When I fail, God's love encourages me to make a better decision next time. We have difficulty understanding that kind of love, because we never have experienced it before!

Another issue is that in today's culture of broken and melded families, an earthly father's love is often absent. New believers who never knew a father's love can have difficulty understanding God the Father's love because of this. But God specifically chose the families He would place us into. With my parents divorcing when I was 10, I spent many formative years without closeness to my father. We would see each other a couple times a year, but even then, it was a challenge for both of us. I won't say that my father did not love me, but what I can say is that at that time, I did not feel it. A cycle had continued, as my father was not close to his father growing up, either. His father left when my Dad was a boy, and it hurt my Dad deeply. Dad's mother had grown up in foster care and never knew her parents. Family brokenness abounds. We sometimes forget how those wounds affect a child, who lacks the logic to figure it out. Most children blame themselves, thinking that adults do not make mistakes.

Certainly, though, my Dad had not felt that unconditional love from his father, the kind that God the Father offers us. When I became a Christian, I also had a strong misconception of what a father's love entails. Some men learn this after they become fathers, just seeing that little baby that came from them. But having no children, I did not learn the lesson there, either. Instead, my understanding of God the Father's love for me, as His child, has been knowledge that seems to grow daily as I learn more about God. My dear friend Todd Williams, who brought me to Jesus, reminded me that my family relationships had been a part of the brokenness that brought me to the Lord. Before knowing the Lord, my love for others was just as incomplete, fractured. Now I see it so differently. Without that brokenness, would I ever have looked to God the Father to fill me with His love? If that is what God used to bring me to Him, how could I look at it as unfair or less than a perfect gift? God changes hearts and today, I know that I never have loved my earthly father more, nor have I ever loved my heavenly Father more. I also know that my father and I are both servants of Jesus. Both of us have been redeemed by the blood of the Lamb. Before I came to Jesus, for many years, I refused to speak to my father, and likely, some of the brokenness my Dad experienced came from my inability to love him in the manner I should have. When driving across the country last year, I stopped to see him for a few days. When I left, I got up at 3:30 a.m. Dad got up with me, walked me to the car and kissed me goodbye. I think I cried for the first two hours of my drive, thanking the Lord for the restoration He had performed in our relationship.

Even though broken families make it more challenging to understand God the Father's love for His children, God does not change. If we only could accept the words of the Bible, where He tells us who He is and how He loves. Instead, I think we approach God with mistrust, daring Him to prove His Word to us. He is up to the challenge.

In the lives of believers, *agape* love should be the norm, not the exception. As our lives are to imitate the life of our Savior, and that is the only kind of love He gave, the bar is high. On the Day of Atonement in the Old Testament times, all of the events pointed forward to Jesus, as He is our High Priest forever. He also became the sin offering, and in addition, was a revelation of the "scapegoat," the one released, as Jesus, the Lamb of God, took away the sins of the world. In the post-AD 70 Jewish world, though, there is no temple, and no more sacrifices. Consequently, on *Yom Kippur* (the Day of Atonement) today, Jews fast and go to their synagogues. On that day, they reflect upon the previous year, thinking of their good deeds and their bad deeds. If a person accomplished more good deeds than bad in that year, they give themselves a passing grade as a good person. More bad deeds than good brings the opposite conclusion – bad person. Yet we know that God does not grade on a curve. He does not compare each of us, and send the bottom 90% to hell and the top 10% to heaven. Instead, our eternal destination is based upon the work of His Son in our lives. Yet even as believers, knowing our destination, we need to remember that God's standard is perfection. *Agape* love, consequently, is not that rare, one-time occurrence that believers should be able to point out. It should be as natural as breathing.

But we cannot love others in this manner without first understanding that this is how God loves us! Additionally, we cannot love others with *agape* love without God dwelling within us, as we are sharing His love with others, not loving under our own power. In the third section of this book, we will discuss how to love others, but here, focus on understanding how God loves us. God's love is not the natural way that any person loves another, no matter how great of a love we might think we have. God is *agape* love!

Part Two: Receiving God's Love

Chapter Three: Abiding in the Vine, Staying Connected!

In the first chapter, I mentioned the significance of John 15 and the passage about abiding in the Vine. After understanding God's *agape* love, abiding in the Vine is how we receive that love. Abide is not a word often-used in today's culture, likely because we change partners, change jobs, change locations and even change churches. How fortunate for babies that they only have to be concerned with changing diapers! But little remains the same. We may still use the terminology that we are to "abide by the law," and most of us realize that refers to obedience, but what does it really mean to abide? Few versions of the Bible even use this old-style word, and instead, choose to replace it with "stay" or "remain." But I am going to continue to abide with "abide," as I think this word conveys so much more. First, let's refresh our thoughts by reading the passage:

[1]"I am the true vine, and My Father is the vinedresser. [2]

Every branch in Me that does not bear fruit He takes away; and every *branch* that bears fruit He prunes, that it may bear more fruit. ³ You are already clean because of the word which I have spoken to you. ⁴ Abide in Me, and I in you. As the branch cannot bear fruit of itself, unless it abides in the vine, neither can you, unless you abide in Me.

⁵ "I am the vine, you *are* the branches. He who abides in Me, and I in him, bears much fruit; for without Me you can do nothing. ⁶ If anyone does not abide in Me, he is cast out as a branch and is withered; and they gather them and throw *them* into the fire, and they are burned. ⁷ If you abide in Me, and My words abide in you, you will ask what you desire, and it shall be done for you. ⁸ By this My Father is glorified, that you bear much fruit; so you will be My disciples.

⁹ "As the Father loved Me, I also have loved you; abide in My love. ¹⁰ If you keep My commandments, you will abide in My love, just as I have kept My Father's commandments and abide in His love.

¹¹ "These things I have spoken to you, that My joy may remain in you, and *that* your joy may be full.
John 15:1-11 (NKJV)

Remember, in an inductive Bible study, the first step is observation, where we ask the typical journalistic questions involving who, what, why, when, where and how, but we do not necessarily answer those questions yet. If this passage is as important as I believe it is, it will not hurt to spend a little extra time observing the passage. Here are some of my observations when I looked at the passage:

• What is fruit?
• Is fruit always good?
• Who does the pruning?
• Who does the work?
• If there is a true vine, is there an untrue vine?
• In John 15:5 it says, "For apart from Me, you can do nothing." If all good works come from God, does that refer to the good works of believers and non-believers? Or is this about something other than good works?

- The Father is the Vinedresser, and He is the one who takes away the branches not bearing fruit; He also is the one who does the pruning.
- Fruit is singular, not plural.
- There are 31 different references to God in this passage with "I," "My," "Father," "Me," "He," and "His."
- A branch does not work hard to produce fruit. The work comes from the Vinedresser.
- Pruning is a natural aspect of gardening to make the garden more fruitful or plentiful.
- Branches produce fruit in season, not all the time!
- These verses were written by John, retelling the words he heard directly from Jesus.
- These were some of the final words that Jesus shared with His disciples before the crucifixion and resurrection, possibly, when on the way to the Garden of Gethsemane.
- Not only do we abide in Jesus, but also, Jesus abides in us!
- We abide in God's *agape* love.
- If we abide in Jesus, He will fill us with His joy. We will have His joy! Joy is the end result of abiding.
- Key words: love (5 times), abide (10 times), fruit (6 times), bear (6 times), branches (4 times), vine (3 times), joy (2 times).

That is a decent observation of the passage, though not all-inclusive. In the next step of an inductive Bible study, interpretation, we bring in other verses with the same key words to help us to understand. One of the questions in the observation section was whether or not this passage was about good works. Other passages in the Bible do not lead us to believe that "fruit" and "good works" are synonymous. Though good works should exist in the life of a believer, good works can also exist in the lives of unbelievers, so this is not necessarily a qualifier for being a Christian. After all, our good works may exemplify the changes God has done in our hearts, but those good works do not earn salvation, which is a free gift. Probably the most important section on fruit is in Galatians:

[22] But the fruit of the Spirit is love, joy, peace, longsuffering,

kindness, goodness, faithfulness, [23] gentleness, self-control. Against such there is no law. [24] And those *who are* Christ's have crucified the flesh with its passions and desires. [25] If we live in the Spirit, let us also walk in the Spirit. [26] Let us not become conceited, provoking one another, envying one another.
Galatians 5:22-26 (NKJV)

Similar to John 15, Galatians 5 discusses the fruit in the life of a believer, and highlights specifically what that fruit entails. Furthermore, we also see mention of us "living in the Spirit" and "walking in the Spirit." Both of these terms reveal God's hope for each believer. God desires for the fruit of the Spirit and a direct attachment to Jesus to be a part of our daily lives, rather than an occasional connection. Notice that when Paul lists the different aspects of the fruit of the Spirit, that it appears to be that all of these should be a part of every believer's life. Instead, when discussing the gifts of the Spirit, we see that God promises at least one gift to each believer. But the fruit of the Spirit encompasses all of those attributes listed in Galatians. Whether or not we use those has to do with how closely we are walking with the Lord!

Many Bible students try to interpret this passage to be about good works. Again, good works should be a part of the life of every believer, yet it is much more than that! Good works should be an outward sign of an inward change. Yet the good works God desires have more to do with our hearts. Are these good works simply trying to earn a reward? Or instead, are our good works something we cannot help but do, in our desire to honor God? Certainly, if our intent is to honor God and love others, those good works have the heart of God involved. But if our good works are to call attention to self, they mean little. Think of a person who bids $5,000 on a worldwide trip at the silent auction for a charity, when the trip is valued at $20,000. Is that good works or a bargain? Jesus gave believers explicit instructions about charity:

[1] "Take heed that you do not do your charitable deeds before men, to be seen by them. Otherwise you have no reward from

58

your Father in heaven. [2] Therefore, when you do a charitable deed, do not sound a trumpet before you as the hypocrites do in the synagogues and in the streets, that they may have glory from men. Assuredly, I say to you, they have their reward. [3] But when you do a charitable deed, do not let your left hand know what your right hand is doing, [4] that your charitable deed may be in secret; and your Father who sees in secret will Himself reward you openly.
Matthew 6:1-4 (NKJV)

Be so secretive that you do not let yourself in on the secret. If we desire praise from men, that is easy to find, especially with social media. But if we desire to please the Lord, our good works will be done with that intent.

As mentioned in the first chapter, another common misinterpretation of this passage is that it is about the Day of Judgment. But notice this verse in John:

> [22] For the Father judges no one, but has committed all judgment to the Son, [23] that all should honor the Son just as they honor the Father. He who does not honor the Son does not honor the Father who sent Him.
> John 5:22-23 (NKJV)

In the Bible, the Judge at the Day of Judgment will be Jesus. If this passage is about judgment, and not encouragement, then why is the Father the one taking away branches and pruning them? Certainly, pruning is not the same as judgment. Jesus identified the Vinedresser as the Father. A key to understanding the whole passage announces our standing as believers, in verse three:

> You are already clean because of the word which I have spoken to you.

That is one of the most important statements in the passage. Jesus cleaned us when He saved us. At the moment we asked Jesus into our hearts and lives as Lord and Savior, repented and asked for His forgiveness, Jesus made us without blemish. Clean as a whistle. We don't have to dust off the dirt because He did that for us already. Jesus took care of our enormous sin debt, as well. We are clean already, spotless! Though His blood washed us white as snow, as believers, the next step involves that daily focus on Jesus. The remainder of this passage in John 15, after understanding that we already are clean, refers to our sanctification, our daily walk with Jesus. If every day we draw closer to Him, every day we imitate Him more, every day we become more of the image of Jesus, then we must be walking closely with Him. In the Old Testament, when Moses went up on the mountain and was in the presence of God, when Moses came back down the mountain, he glowed! As believers, the more time we spend with Jesus, the more others can look at us and know that we have been in the presence of the Lord. Even when Moses came down the mountain, his heart was still with the Lord. To not leave God's side and to walk with Him is to abide. Abide is about relationship. Without being connected to the Vine, a branch cannot produce fruit, and those with some gardening experience will understand that a branch does not work hard to produce that fruit. The work comes from the Vinedresser and includes a healthy Vine. The fruit on the branch is a natural progression from the work of the Vinedresser and the attachment to the Vine.

Certainly, if that branch becomes separated from the Vine, it is just a dead stick on the ground. If it had any fruit attached, the fruit would quickly wither and die, as well. Additionally, notice the presence of the Trinity in this passage. Jesus is the Vine, the Father is the Vinedresser, and we also see a discussion of fruit, which points to the fruit of the Holy Spirit. John seems to be very concerned with abiding as about half the times "abide" is used in the Bible, it comes from John. Here's another key verse:

> I have written to you, fathers,
> Because you have known Him who is from the beginning.
> I have written to you, young men,
> Because you are strong, and the word of God abides in you,

And you have overcome the wicked one.
1 John 2:14 (NKJV)

What does it mean for the "word of God" to abide in us? Some might argue whether or not this verse is referring to Jesus living within a believer or a believer following an admonition written by James:

But be doers of the word, and not hearers only, deceiving yourselves.
James 1:22 (NKJV)

If the words of the Bible are abiding in us, then we will not just know the Word, but live the Word. John gave Jesus the title of the "Word" in John 1, so just as easily, this could be speaking of Jesus abiding within us. Why does it have to be one or the other? If Jesus dwells within us, then His Words dwell within us, too. If we truly believe what we claim to believe, then our walks with the Lord are transforming experiences! As Paul reminded us in Romans 12, when we present our bodies as living sacrifices, diligently protecting ourselves from being conformed to the ways of the world and instead being transformed to the ways of the Word, we are abiding. That passage in Romans 12 also points out that it is "reasonable" to do this, not over and above the call of duty. Abiding in Jesus is loving Him back for all He has done for us. How can we know if Jesus is abiding in us, or if we are abiding in Him?

Whoever confesses that Jesus is the Son of God, God abides in him, and he in God.
1 John 4:15 (NKJV)

It certainly would appear that both are happening. We also see in this verse that confessing is different than just believing. Confessing is an action verb:

[9] that if you confess with your mouth Jesus as Lord, and believe in your heart that God raised Him from the dead, you will be saved; [10] for with the heart a person believes, resulting

in righteousness, and with the mouth he confesses, resulting in salvation.
Romans 10:9-10 (NKJV)

Confession brings salvation and belief brings righteousness, according to this statement of Paul in Romans. Jesus, through the writings of John, gives us another interesting aspect of abiding in Him:

> [31] Then Jesus said to those Jews who believed Him, "If you abide in My word, you are My disciples indeed. [32] And you shall know the truth, and the truth shall make you free."
> John 8:31-32 (NKJV)

To be a follower of Christ, we must abide in His word. That involves reading it, for a start. How many Christians only listen to a pastor speak on Sunday mornings, and would not know the difference if the pastor either misquoted or misinterpreted the passage? To abide in the Word is to always be in the Word. Life comes from the eternal, living Word of God. If I was in a relationship with a woman, and wrote her a letter from my heart to her heart, but she would not read the letter, could she really love me? God's letter to us was written in the crimson blood of Jesus. His Word gives us all we need to know to maneuver life on this earth. Do you want to be a disciple of Jesus? Then abide in His word. IF we abide in His word, THEN we shall know the truth. IF we know the truth, THEN the truth will set us free!

Abiding is not a new term in the New Testament. Let's look at an example from the Old Testament:

> Lord, who may abide in Your tabernacle?
> Who may dwell in Your holy hill?
> Psalm 15:1 (NKJV)

Often in the Psalms, and in Hebrew poetry, we see "echoes." The second line is a restatement of the first line, using different words. That is exactly what we see here in Psalm 15. Abiding in God's tabernacle and dwelling in His holy hill are one and the same. Abiding is not a visit or brief stop-over. Nor is it as simple as staying or remaining. To abide entails every aspect of our lives.

At least in this passage, abide and dwell are used synonymously. The end of Psalm 23 is a beautiful picture of abiding, but instead, we see the word dwell:

> Surely goodness and mercy shall follow me
> All the days of my life;
> And I will dwell in the house of the Lord Forever.
> Psalm 23:6 (NKJV)

Forever! That should give us a different perspective of "abide," for as believers, we will dwell in His house for eternity, with God's goodness and God's mercy following every one of our steps. Sometimes, we put such a huge emphasis on this earth and our lives here. But we are just passing through. But because Jesus abides in us now, and we abide in Him, we are seated (past tense) in the heavens with Jesus, according to Ephesians 2:6. God does not see us as residents of earth, as our citizenship is already in heaven. This brings the admonition of Jesus to a new level to not "be of this world." Why would we allow ourselves to be tied to this broken, sinful earth when we already are "seated in the heavens," with our citizenship there? We also see in Psalm 91:1 that we dwell in the secret place of the Most High God, and abide under the shadow of the Almighty. When we think of the immensity of God, the shadow beneath Him is equally immense! That verse speaks of the relationship between our abiding in Him and God's protection of His children.

In Psalm 51, King David prayed to the Lord to "take not Your Holy Spirit from me." In the Old Testament, the Holy Spirit filled believers for a time or season, but for post-resurrection believers, the Holy Spirit never will leave us. Jesus said,

> [15] "If you love Me, you will keep My commandments.
> [16] I will ask the Father, and He will give you another Helper, that He may be with you forever; [17] *that is* the Spirit of truth,

whom the world cannot receive, because it does not see Him or know Him, *but* you know Him because He abides with you and will be in you. [18] "I will not leave you as orphans; I will come to you.
John 14:15-18 (NASB)

The Holy Spirit abides within each believer, and never will leave us or forsake us. The passage begins by speaking of how we can demonstrate our love for Jesus. Obedience to the Lord is how we can love Him back. Certainly, we all know that He loved us first, and if we can even begin to grasp the depth of God's love for us, His children, and what He has accomplished on our behalves, our desire rightly and reasonably would be to love Him back. By honoring His Laws, we do that. But all of us realize how difficult it is to follow the Law when we still have a sin nature and we are surrounded by a sinful world. Yet because God abides in us, we are not on our own. Jesus and the Holy Spirit live within us, and abide within us.

If we abide in Jesus, we remain with Him, in Him, by Him and through Him. Loving Him back in obedience is how we abide in Him. Each day, we are faced with decisions whether to do it God's way or the world's way. Instead of "doing what is right in our own eyes," we are called to "do what is right in God's eyes." Before we knew Jesus, we were slaves to sin, but as believers, we are slaves to righteousness, and sin becomes a choice rather than just a natural progression. We can either run to sin and glorify Satan or run away from sin and glorify God. (Think of Joseph running from Potiphar's wife). Running away from sin involves relying on God's power within us, the Holy Spirit. The Greek word for power is *dunamis*, where we get the word dynamite. This power is explosive! This battle wages within us many times each day, whether to walk in the Spirit or walk in the flesh. If we walk in the flesh, we cannot please God. Listen! With God dwelling within us, when we are considering sin, He does not remain silent. But sometimes, we choose not to listen. That is where repentance must continue in each of our lives. Having the opportunity to repent continues to point to God's love, as there is no condemnation in Jesus Christ.

64

In the Bible, the best example of God's love is the cross, for when we understand what Jesus did for us, we cannot question that love. There we go back to *agape*! Likely, the second-best example of God's love is His relationship with His chosen people, the children of Israel. In the Old Testament, we see a repetitive cycle, where the Jews honored God, fell into idolatry, God punished them, they returned to God, they fell into idolatry...and the cycle kept spinning 'round and 'round. Finally, God sent the northern tribes into captivity with the Assyrians, and Judah entered captivity with the Babylonians. It did not end there, either. After 70 years, those in Babylonian captivity were allowed to return, though many remained in Babylon and chose not to return. Years later, when the Jews did not acknowledge Jesus as Messiah, God sent them to the four corners of the earth. Still, it does not end there. In Revelation, we see that God once again will focus on the Jews and will bring many to salvation. God does not turn His back on His children! Even with the example of the children of Israel, we see the Jews turning their backs on Him. We also see much sin, especially idolatry. Yet God and God's love are faithful. Because He loves us, He punishes us, but again, it is not a trip to the woodshed. Instead, God's punishment is loving, edifying and teaching, helping us to walk in a manner worthy of our calling. God is much more forgiving than we are. Our weaknesses and limitations are why we have the tendency of looking at Him as a God who punishes instantly.

Earlier (in chapter one), I pointed out the meaning of the Greek words, mistranslated in John 15 by translators as "takes away" and "prunes," causing many to believe this passage is about God's judgment on believers who are walking in sin. Those are weak interpretations that send us down the wrong path, as the Greek word translated as "takes away" here is actually translated as "lifts up" in a majority of its uses throughout the Bible. "Lifts up" makes perfect sense with the actions of a Vinedresser in a vineyard. When the Vinedresser sees branches on the ground, He lifts them out of the dirt to help them grow more healthily. This is about encouragement, not judgment or discipline. We also know that pruning is a natural part of growth. We prune a branch to help it grow stronger and produce more fruit. After a branch of roses blooms with 10 beautiful roses, we prune the branch, and in no time at all, instead of putting its energy into the dead blooms, that branch is gloriously blooming once again. Many people somehow equate the word "pruning" with God painfully disciplining us. When is the last time you heard a branch scream, "Ouch," when you pruned it to help it grow more abundantly? We also can know that this section of John 15 is not about unbelievers, and God's judgment upon them. For these branches are "in the Vine," which tells us that they are attached to the Vine, attached to Jesus!

Others think this passage is about believers who lose their salvation if they do not "abide in the Vine." First of all, salvation is a gift rather than something that we have earned with our behavior or works. The Bible makes that point clear.

> He saved us, not on the basis of deeds which we have done in righteousness, but according to His mercy, by the washing of regeneration and renewing by the Holy Spirit,
> Titus 3:5 (NKJV)

Is it possible for a believer to lose his salvation? With a number of verses stating the contrary, it sounds like Jesus loves us so much He will not let go of us! How could it be "eternal life" if we could lose it?

> but whoever drinks of the water that I will give him shall never thirst; but the water that I will give him will become in him a well of water springing up to eternal life."
> John 4:14 (NKJV)

> [27] "My sheep hear My voice, and I know them, and they follow Me; [28] and I give eternal life to them, and they will never perish; and no one will snatch them out of My hand.
> John 10:27-28 (NKJV)

> [9] Much more then, having now been justified by His blood, we shall be saved from the wrath of God through Him. [10] For if while we were enemies we were reconciled to God through

the death of His Son, much more, having been reconciled, we shall be saved by His life.
Romans 5:9-10 (NKJV)

[35] Who will separate us from the love of Christ? Will tribulation, or distress, or persecution, or famine, or nakedness, or peril, or sword? [36] Just as it is written, "For Your sake we are being put to death all day long; We were considered as sheep to be slaughtered." [37] But in all these things we overwhelmingly conquer through Him who loved us. [38] For I am convinced that neither death, nor life, nor angels, nor principalities, nor things present, nor things to come, nor powers, [39] nor height, nor depth, nor any other created thing, will be able to separate us from the love of God, which is in Christ Jesus our Lord.
Romans 8:35-39 (NKJV)

If it were all about our power, we would be in trouble. But if we are in the hands of Jesus, and in His Father's hands, who can pry us loose? As badly as Satan would like to do exactly that, he is simply a created thing, an angel that departed from heaven. Regardless of whether or not he falls into the category of angel or any other created thing, we have been assured that Satan cannot separate us from the love of Christ! When it says nothing can separate us, what does nothing mean? Pretty easy, as it means NO THING, NOTHING!

But we cannot lose what we never had. If you have not received the salvation that Jesus offers, then you must first be attached to the Vine to have any of the blessings John speaks of in this passage. This passage is so strongly about God's blessings, rather than His judgment. Again, God does chastise His children, but that in itself is a blessing. If He didn't love us, why would our improvement matter to Him?

When I think of the sin in my life as a believer, more than God's punishment, I remember my lack of joy. It seems that joy comes from obedience, and we know that the joy of the Lord is our strength. At the end of this spectacular and important passage on

67

abiding in the Vine, we see this statement from Jesus:

> "These things I have spoken to you, that My joy may remain in you, and *that* your joy may be full.
> John 15:11 (NKJV)

It's all about joy. If we keep that relationship with Jesus, and connection to the Vine, then His joy will permeate us, and His joy will become our joy! The abundance that God wants to give us is an abundance of joy. Do not make the mistake of following "prosperity Gospel" pastors who will tell you that God wants to give you an abundance of money. God will not buy you with money, as He has purchased you with His blood! Satan, on the other hand, will get you to sell your soul for a pittance of its value. God's abundance of joy testifies of who God is as even in the most difficult circumstance, we still can have the joy of the LORD as our strength. Have you ever met a bitter Christian? Bitterness either comes from a lack of belief or a lack of obedience. If we believe the words of the Bible, and trust God, we will follow Him through our obedience, and know that His promises either have come true or will come true. And our joy? It will be full! What an amazing promise!

Chapter Four: Amen and the Authority of Jesus

Abiding in the Lord Jesus should be a constant in the life of a believer, but there will be an ebb and flow in the lives of every believer abiding in the Lord. The best news for us is that there will not be an ebb and flow with Jesus abiding in us. Occasionally, when I am dining in a restaurant, I notice an older couple at an adjacent table. Sometimes, during the course of the meal, not one word is spoken. It could be that there is nothing left to be said, after all the years, or that even though they are together, their relationship is out of necessity rather than choice. At the same time, I have noticed older couples walking hand-in-hand down the beach, and regardless of age or years spent together, they have done something to keep the honeymoon going. I often have thought that our relationships with Jesus should be just like that. Relationships remain exciting when we do not get stuck in ruts. In my college years, a local performer sang a song with these lyrics, "A groove is a rut, a dent in the ground.

You get in that rut and go around and around. A rut is a ditch before too long, and a ditch is a grave with two ends gone. So, look out for the groove!" There is something comforting about repetition, but if that repetition becomes too mindless, we might be repeating the action for the wrong reason.

To abide in Jesus, and have our (*agape*) love for Him continue to grow, we need to fall in love with His Word. For it is God's Word where we learn more about the Father, more about Jesus and more about the Holy Spirit. Again, this should be heart knowledge, rather than head knowledge, even if it might begin in the head. Once we have a deeper understanding of God's *agape* love, we learn to abide with Him, in Him, and through Him. Think of abiding as a long, intimate walk, so long it is unending. God created each of us, and we are unique. Imagine as we walk with Jesus, He wants us to reveal our unique quality to Him, and while doing so, we get to learn more profound truths about Him, as well. To me, though the Bible is lengthy, it is not unknowable. No matter how many times I read it, my perspective can change on any given day when I see a verse so differently than ever before.

> For the word of God is living and active and sharper than any two-edged sword, and piercing as far as the division of soul and spirit, of both joints and marrow, and able to judge the thoughts and intentions of the heart.
> Hebrews 4:12 (NASB)

We think of words as finite, but God's Word is so dynamic that we will continue to learn and to grow when we spend time reading His Word. But it should not be an item on a checklist. "Today, I am going to read two chapters." If we are simply doing it to cross a chore off the list, instead of trying to apply the words to our lives, we are missing out. If we meditate on God's Word day and night, as it says to do in Psalm 1:2, then even after we have read verses, we will chew on those verses throughout the day. Many people attempt to read through the Bible each year. January 1, each year, they start once again in Genesis 1. It's not a bad plan, but after doing that for a few years, it would also be a blessing to slow down and spend more time on each word. One of my favorite ways of reading the Bible is to start in Genesis, and try to find Jesus on each page. Yes, the Old Testament occurred before Jesus came to earth as 100% man and 100% God. Yet in the Old Testament, we can see examples or models of Jesus. For example, we can see Jesus in the story of Abraham taking Isaac to Mt. Moriah to sacrifice his son. If you have trouble seeing that, email me and I will be glad to point it out to you!

We can see Jesus in the first verse of the Old Testament:

> In the beginning God created the heavens and the earth.
> Genesis 1:1 (NKJV)

Actually, it does not say "in the beginning." In Hebrew, it says "in beginning," which is a better interpretation. "In the beginning," almost would lead us to believe that there was a moment when God began to exist, but instead, He pre-existed eternally. "In beginning," instead, demonstrates a process that He began, and in Genesis, that process God began was creation. He created all for man, and then created man. Similarly, God prepared the Promised Land for the Jews before they entered, and we also know that Jesus departed the earth to prepare a place for believers! In this first verse, in the first mention of God, it is the Hebrew word "*Elohim.*" That Hebrew suffix of "*im*" denotes male and plural. So, in beginning, God (plural) created! "Created" with this Hebrew word *bara* means created something out of nothing, which is quite different than a carpenter building a table from scrap lumber. God, plural, created the heavens and the earth out of nothing. How can God be singular and have a plural suffix? Well, the Trinity would explain that. And there's Jesus in the first verse!

In addition to seeing Jesus on each page, another interesting and important way to go through the Bible is to look for God's promises. Those promises fall into three categories:
- Promises that have been fulfilled already.
- Promises that have not been fulfilled already.
- Promises that have been fulfilled already and will also be fulfilled again.

When we see promises that have been fulfilled, they remind us that our God is faithful. He cannot lie, and knowing this, in our personal walks with Jesus, our faith grows. We can put His promises in the bank. If He has not let us down before, and we continue to see His faithfulness, it becomes easier to trust Him the longer we walk with Jesus! It is interesting that one of the Hebrew words used for "faithful" is *aman* (אָמַן).

> Thus says the Lord, the Redeemer of Israel *and* its Holy One,
> To the despised One,
> To the One abhorred by the nation,
> To the Servant of rulers,
> "Kings will see and arise,
> Princes will also bow down,
> Because of the Lord who is faithful, the Holy One of Israel
> who has chosen You."
> Isaiah 49:7 (NASB)

Here is another Old Testament example:

> "Know therefore that the Lord your God, He is God, the faithful God, who keeps His covenant and His lovingkindness to a thousandth generation with those who love Him and keep His commandments;
> Deuteronomy 7:9 (NASB)

Again, in the verses quoted above, *aman* has been translated as "faithful," and we can know that our God is a faithful God. The Hebrew language does not have vowels. Consequently, the words *aman* and *amen* are written exactly the same. As Christians, we are much more familiar with the word *amen*! *Amen* is one of the rare words that seems to be the same in almost every language – Hebrew, Greek, Latin, English, German, French and Italian, to name a few. At the end of a prayer, we might say *Amen*, and by doing so, what we are really adding is our agreement of "so be it." Let it be said, and let it be done. But another way of looking at that word is by once again focusing on the Hebrew meaning of faithful. *Amen* at the end of a prayer is stating our belief that because God is faithful, He will

72

answer our prayers in His will. Just as in the prayers of Jesus to the Father, our desire is for the Father's will and for His answers to be in accordance with that will. Consequently, we trust His faithfulness to accomplish His will in our lives.

Interestingly, we also can see that "*Amen*" is a title of Christ in Revelation:

> "And to the angel of the church of the Laodiceans write, 'These things says the Amen, the Faithful and True Witness, the Beginning of the creation of God:
> Revelation 3:14 (NKJV)

In the New Testament, specifically in the Gospel of John, Jesus often states, "*Amen, amen*" at the beginning of a verse. In different translations of the Bible, this could instead say, "Verily, verily," or "truly, truly," or even "most assuredly," but the word is actually *Amen.* There seems to be a stark difference between a verse beginning with that word, especially when uttered by Jesus, and a verse ending with that word. Additionally, repetitive words in the Bible are attention getters. It is almost like, "Hey, all that is written is important, but when I say this word twice, you need to pay extra close attention!" I think in terms of stop, look and listen. "*Amen, amen*" points to a solemn pronouncement made by Jesus, but in addition, when looking closely at these statements in the Gospel of John, they also seem to be Jesus speaking with authority. Here is an example:

> Therefore Jesus answered and was saying to them, "Truly, truly (*amen-amen*), I say to you, the Son can do nothing of Himself, unless it is something He sees the Father doing; for whatever the Father does, these things the Son also does in like manner.
> John 5:19 (NASB)

I always am amazed when people state that Jesus never declared to be God. Instead, Jesus made this claim many times, and when reading the Bible, if we do not see that, all we need to do is to see the reaction of the Pharisees when Jesus speaks. The Pharisees were frequently offended by His statements, as the Pharisees completely understood that Jesus was claiming to be God. In fact, that is why they put Him to death, as they thought His statements were heretical. In this passage quoted above, Jesus stated that He is incapable of acting without the power and intent of the Father, as He came directly from the Father. In this "*amen-amen*" statement, we see the authority of Jesus, given by the Father. Here's another example that might bring this home:

> ⁵⁷ So the Jews said to Him, "You are not yet fifty years old, and have You seen Abraham?" ⁵⁸ Jesus said to them, "Truly, truly (*amen-amen*), I say to you, before Abraham was born, I am." ⁵⁹ Therefore they picked up stones to throw at Him, but Jesus hid Himself and went out of the temple.
> John 8:57-59 (NASB)

Notice the specific words here that Jesus certainly chose carefully. Before Abraham was, I AM! He is claiming to be the I AM of the Old Testament. Why else did they pick up stones, wanting to kill Him? To connect the dots, let's go to the burning bush:

> ¹³ Then Moses said to God, "Indeed, *when* I come to the children of Israel and say to them, 'The God of your fathers has sent me to you,' and they say to me, 'What *is* His name?' what shall I say to them?"
> ¹⁴ And God said to Moses, "I AM WHO I AM." And He said, "Thus you shall say to the children of Israel, 'I AM has sent me to you.'
> Exodus 3:13-14 (NKJV)

I AM is a title of God, the name of God! When Moses asked God for His name, God gave His name. I AM. When Jesus stated this to the Jews, they wanted to stone Him. They certainly understood exactly what Jesus was saying. He claimed to be God, and in so doing, was announcing His authority as God. To understand the power of "I AM," let's look at one other interesting passage in the Gospel of John:

¹ When Jesus had spoken these words, He went forth with His disciples over the ravine of the Kidron, where there was a garden, in which He entered with His disciples. ² Now Judas also, who was betraying Him, knew the place, for Jesus had often met there with His disciples. ³ Judas then, having received the *Roman* cohort and officers from the chief priests and the Pharisees, came there with lanterns and torches and weapons. ⁴ So Jesus, knowing all the things that were coming upon Him, went forth and said to them, "Whom do you seek?" ⁵ They answered Him, "Jesus the Nazarene." He said to them, "I am *He*." And Judas also, who was betraying Him, was standing with them. ⁶ So when He said to them, "I am *He*," they drew back and fell to the ground.
John 18:1-6 (NASB)

When we see an italicized word in a Bible verse, those italics either refer to a quoted verse or an added word. For example, when the New Testament has a sentence all in italics, it would be a verse quoted directly from the Old Testament. But when we see one or two words italicized, instead, it shows that the translators added a word or two to help the verse make sense in our language. In this passage from John 18, after acknowledging that He is indeed Jesus of Nazareth, whom they were seeking, Jesus stated, "I AM." Jesus did not say, "I am He." The translators might have tried to make this statement make sense in English, but instead, by adding "He", they have changed its intended meaning. We can see the effect that Jesus' claim had. He was not just announcing Himself as God. His words also carried the power of God. When He said, "I AM," they fell to the ground. God created all with His breath, and simply by breathing His name, I AM, they fell over like bowling pins! That is authority!

In John 6, we see another of the *"amen-amen"* statements:

⁴⁷ Most assuredly (*amen-amen*), I say to you, he who believes in Me has everlasting life. ⁴⁸ I am the bread of life. ⁴⁹ Your fathers ate the manna in the wilderness, and are dead. ⁵⁰ This is the bread which comes down from heaven, that one may eat of it and not die. ⁵¹ I am the living bread which came

down from heaven. If anyone eats of this bread, he will live forever; and the bread that I shall give is My flesh, which I shall give for the life of the world."
John 6:47-51 (NKJV)

This verse speaks of more than mere belief. This belief may begin with an intellectual understanding of the claims of Jesus, but more importantly, saving knowledge in Jesus Christ involves placing our trust in Him. This reliance is easy to distinguish from just belief, as we know that even the demons believe and tremble (James 2:19). If we rely upon Jesus, that also would involve taking Him at His Word, and also the understanding that Jesus has the authority to make those statements. This brings us back to the Bible, for if we as believers do not read His Word, how can we rely upon it? To me, it is a step-by-step process. First, we must read the Bible. It does not stop there. We can re-read the Bible forever and not learn all there is to know. In fact, the more I know, I realize that I know less. That head knowledge needs to travel 18 inches to the heart, so we live the words of Jesus. Without relying on God's Word, His Laws and His statements, we are not trusting Him. Trusting in God is saving knowledge of Jesus Christ. In this statement, Jesus also drew a correlation between the *manna* given to the Jews as sustenance, during their 40 years in the wilderness, and the fulfillment of that Old Testament gift, when Jesus came as the "bread of life." The sustenance that Jesus offers is all-encompassing, but without eating His Word, what is the point? When we eat His Word, it goes from outside to the inside!

In the Old Testament, men were called to keep the Law of God, and God gave men the sacrificial system to cover their sin. Yet this was an arduous process. With the death and resurrection of Jesus, Jesus not only covered all sin but also, took away that sin from believers. Galatians 3:24-25 reminds us that the Law was a tutor to bring us to Christ Jesus. The Law, however, does not go away. One of the greatest gifts to believers is that if Jesus dwells within us, we are no longer slaves to sin. We still sin, sadly, but each sin is a choice rather than a natural reaction. In Romans 7:15, Paul reminded us that what he hates he continues to do. If Paul still struggled with sin with his depth of relationship with the Lord and knowledge of the Lord, I think it is certain that the rest of us will have similar struggles. Here is another interesting *"amen-amen"* statement:

> Truly, truly (*amen-amen*), I say to you, if anyone keeps My word he will never see death."
> John 8:51 (NASB)

But again, no one can completely keep the Word of Jesus, can they? When we look at this verse in context, Jesus is speaking to the Pharisees. As always, the Pharisees are trying to trap Him in His words, but imagine, trapping the Word of God with the Word of God! Jesus will not incorrectly state anything. What Jesus is offering them here is eternal life, if they will just believe on Him. Sadly, the Pharisees had become so self-righteous they lost sight of the reason for the prophesied Messiah. Instead of understanding that the Messiah came to save lost souls, the Pharisees believed they already had received salvation through their own adherence to God's Laws. In addition, they added to the laws God had given. Their incorrect logic thought, "more law, more righteousness." But no one can save themselves. Self righteousness did not die with the Pharisees. We still have Christian denominations today that believe we earn salvation through our actions. Some of those actions include church attendance, placing an offering in the collection plate, repetitious prayers and good works. Sadly, instead of focusing on the grace of God, some even state that grace only will cover those rare instances when we have not earned salvation, kind of a "gap insurance."

This points to the human condition. The Bible speaks strongly against pride, and it is pride that makes us want to believe that there is something wonderful about us that makes us better than others. Truly, all denominations have a touch of this, as we all want to believe that we are members of the most exclusive club. We want to be right. But we should not be so sure of ourselves that we set ourselves up for a very dangerous fall. It is my belief that when we get to heaven, each one of us will discover doctrines that we misunderstood. But be careful that your misunderstood doctrine is not salvation based. Do you honestly think there will be a street of mansions in heaven segregated by denominations, skin colors, or doctrines? "Well, of course, I live on Presbyterian Avenue, as do my fellow Presbyterians." How ridiculous to think that Jesus did it all to create unity…one church, one body and one heart, but then would separate us into divisive factions. Salvation is a gift, and gifts are given, not earned. Jesus did it all. He gave it all and accomplished it all for us. Receive His salvation, and walk it out by obedience to God and God's Law. Adherence to the Law is not to gain righteousness, but a simple way of loving God back.

The Gospel of John includes 25 of those statements that Jesus begins by stating, "*Amen, amen.*" Many of those statements are reported by Matthew, Mark and Luke, but interestingly, none of the other Gospel writers use that same terminology of "*amen, amen.*" These verses are certainly worth reading. I am including a chart here to make your study of these a little easier.

#	Bible Verse	Paraphrase of that verse
1	John 1:51	Heaven opens with angels ascending and descending upon the Son of Man.
2	John 3:3	Must be born again to see the kingdom of God.
3	John 3:5	Must be born of water and the Spirit to enter the kingdom of God.
4	John 3:11	We can speak and testify of God without receiving Him.
5	John 5:19	The Son can do nothing apart from the Father. Jesus does what the Father does.
6	John 5:24	He who hears the words of Jesus and believes on the Father has everlasting life.
7	John 5:25	The hour has arrived when the dead shall hear the words of Jesus and pass from death to life.
8	John 6:26	Jesus said that people were seeking Him not because of the miracles but because Jesus filled them with bread.
9	John 6:32	Moses gave *manna*, but the Father gives the true bread of heaven

#	Bible Verse	Paraphrase of that verse
10	John 6:47	He that believes on Jesus will have everlasting life.
11	John 6:53	Only by eating of Jesus' flesh, and drinking of His blood, can we have His life in us!
12	John 8:34	Anyone who sins is a servant to sin.
13	John 8:51	If we follow the words of Jesus, we never will see death.
14	John 8:58	Before Abraham existed, Jesus was I AM!
15	John 10:1	Anyone who does not enter through the door of the sheepfold is a thief.
16	John 10:7	Jesus gives an I AM statement, saying, I AM the door of the sheep
17	John 12:24	When corn or wheat dies, its seed produces much fruit!
18	John 13:16	A servant is not greater than his master, nor is he who is sent greater than he who sent him.
19	John 13:20	If we receive those sent by Jesus, we receive Jesus. If we receive Jesus, we receive the Father who sent Jesus.
20	John 13:21	Here, Jesus states that one of His disciples will betray Him.
21	John 13:38	After Peter brags about how much he loves Jesus, Jesus tells Peter that before the cock crows, Peter will deny Jesus three times.
22	John 14:12	If we believe on Jesus, we will do greater works than Jesus after His return to heaven.
23	John 16:20	Jesus reminds His disciples that they will weep, but the world will rejoice and their weeping will turn to joy.
24	John 16:23	Whatever we ask of the Father in the name of Jesus, the Father will give us!
25	John 21:18	Jesus tells Peter, when you were young, you dressed yourself and went where you wanted. When old, you will stretch out your hands.

Jesus is the *Alpha* and the *Omega*, according to Revelation 1:18 and Revelation 22:13, with *alpha* being the first letter of the Greek alphabet and *omega* being the last letter. So, in this book so far, we have journeyed together through a few words beginning with that *alpha* – *agape*, abide and *amen*. That takes us to another, authority! We began by discussing God's *agape* love, and without understanding His love, capable of transforming us, we really cannot know God. How could anyone know God unless God allowed us to know Him? Without His desire for a personal relationship with us, God is unreachable and unknowable. Know God, know peace. No God, no peace! To know God is to know His love, and as that love changes us, we begin to walk with Him, to abide in Him. As we abide in Him, and He abides in us, this becomes a journey in tandem. Then, *amen* becomes a part of it. When we pronounce *amen* at the end of a prayer, we are in agreement with God, in agreement with what His Word teaches us. When we pray in the name of Jesus, we are asking for God to bring everything to fruition that He says. (Whether we agree or not, His will certainly will be done anyway!) But our lives are prayers to Him, as believers, if we are abiding in the Vine. Attached to Jesus, we remain in agreement with His will in our lives. Yet we also are able to see that in the "verily, verily;" "truly, truly; "most assuredly" statements, which are actually "*amen, amen*," that when Jesus began speaking with this phrase, He was speaking with authority. That authority was God-given.

Sometimes, we get confused when thinking about God being one and in three persons. Does Jesus live inside of each believer, or God the Father or God the Holy Spirit? Yes! Did God the Father create the universe or Jesus? Yes! With the oneness of God, the three parts of God cannot be separated. Yet there is order. We see a great representation of order in the military. There are colonels outranked by generals, and some of those colonels are actually more intelligent, more compassionate and more experienced than the generals. Yet we salute the general, not for the man he is, but for his rank. In the same manner, throughout the life of Jesus on this earth, we can see that Jesus did everything in the Father's will, to glorify the Father and to please the Father. Was this because the Father was more powerful than Jesus? No! They are both God! If both are all powerful, omnipotent, how could one be more powerful than the other, when all-powerful means there is no lack of any power? In the same manner, the Holy Spirit always testifies of Jesus and points to Jesus. Is the Holy Spirit less powerful than Jesus? No! Again, the Holy Spirit is also all-powerful. The best explanation I have heard is not the classic one, that an egg has three parts, as the shell, yellow and white are all parts of the egg. Instead, the best explanation is math. $1 + 1 + 1 = 3$ but $1 \times 1 \times 1 = 1$! Three parts, equal, and omnipotent, omniscient and omnipresent, in order. In Ephesians, Paul did not tell wives to submit to husbands because men are more important to God than women. Instead, again, with submission, we see order, in the same way that Jesus submitted to the will of the Father.

When Jesus spoke these words, with the authority coming from the Father, and the words to glorify the Father, He also was claiming to be God. This was offensive to the Pharisees, as they wanted to be the gods of the Jewish world, and certainly enjoyed their self-appointed power. Yet in the life of a believer, it is not until we desire to submit our lives to the authority of Jesus that our walk with Him will have His power. When we walk to appease our own desires, that power is our own. When we walk to glorify Jesus, and submit to His authority in our lives, our walks are Jesus-powered. Dying to self means that our lives exist through Jesus. Our desires are gone, and our hearts coincide with the heart of Jesus. Let's look at some of the Bible verses that speak of the authority of Jesus and start with one that speaks volumes:

> [1] So He got into a boat, crossed over, and came to His own city. [2] Then behold, they brought to Him a paralytic lying on a bed. When Jesus saw their faith, He said to the paralytic, "Son, be of good cheer; your sins are forgiven you." [3] And at once some of the scribes said within themselves, "This Man blasphemes!"
> Matthew 9:1-3 (NKJV)

The scribes were teachers of the Law. They rightly deduced that only God could forgive sin, and by doing so, Jesus was claiming to be God. This made me try to think of Old Testament, prophetic

81

Scriptures that not only spoke of a coming Messiah, but claimed that the Messiah would be God. This is one example:

> [5] "Behold, *the* days are coming," says the Lord,
> "That I will raise to David a Branch of righteousness;
> A King shall reign and prosper,
> And execute judgment and righteousness in the earth.
> [6] In His days Judah will be saved,
> And Israel will dwell safely;
> Now this *is* His name by which He will be called:
> THE LORD OUR RIGHTEOUSNESS
> Jeremiah 23:5-6 (NKJV)

Who else could the "LORD our righteousness" be, as no man is righteous of himself? Certainly, the Pharisees also understood the correlation between "branch" and Messiah, as a branch would bring new life to the line of David. We could see this specifically in Isaiah 11:

> [1] There shall come forth a Rod from the stem of Jesse,
> And a Branch shall grow out of his roots.
> [2] The Spirit of the Lord shall rest upon Him,
> The Spirit of wisdom and understanding,
> The Spirit of counsel and might,
> The Spirit of knowledge and of the fear of the Lord.
> Isaiah 11:1-2 (NKJV)

King David, the son of Jesse, is obviously the "stem of Jesse." The Branch, the Messiah, was to come from the roots of David's family. In Hebrew, the word Nazareth (נצרי) means "branch," as even the hometowns of Jesus had prophetic names. Bethlehem means "house of bread." The "Bread of Life" and the "Branch" had close ties to Bethlehem and Nazareth. Nothing is a coincidence! Another nugget in this verse brings to mind some assorted verses in Revelation. In Revelation 1:4, 3:1, 4:5 and 5:6 there are references to the seven Spirits of God. In this verse from Isaiah, is this an example of the seven Spirits of God in Isaiah 11:2?

    1. The Spirit of the Lord

2. The Spirit of wisdom
3. The Spirit of understanding
4. The Spirit of counsel
5. The Spirit of might
6. The Spirit of knowledge
7. The Spirit of the fear of the Lord

For Jeremiah to identify the Branch, the Messiah, with the name "The LORD our righteousness," it would appear that the Pharisees should have known that the Messiah would be God. Yet lest we forget, Jesus told His disciples that He would die and would rise again in three days (Matthew 16:21), but even with those words to prepare them, when Jesus was crucified, they were distraught, rather than looking for the resurrected Jesus three days later. Sometimes, we can ignore the most obvious warnings. Whether or not the scribes and Pharisees understood that the coming Messiah would be God, they were not prepared for His offer of salvation. Though for those not steeped in the Law, clouding their beliefs, this is difficult to imagine. Consider the lame man Jesus healed on the Sabbath. What would have been more memorable to you…seeing a lame man rise up and walk or that someone had illegally done work on the Sabbath?

On a trip to Israel, I got in the elevator on Saturday, the Jewish Sabbath, and though the elevator was in a high-rise hotel, I was unable to push a button. Instead, the elevator automatically stopped on each floor, ensuring that by pushing a button we were not working on the Sabbath. Jesus challenged their tunnel vision. Retold in Matthew 12, He asked them if their sheep fell into a pit on the Sabbath, would they save the life of the sheep or let it die, making sure to not do work on the Sabbath? Isn't the sanctity of a life, even an animal's life, more important? These miracles of such a humble man, nothing ever seen before, should have been much more eye-opening than whether or not the healing occurred on the Sabbath! Certainly, we can see why Jesus wept over Jerusalem (Luke 19), as the people He came to save were spiritually blind. Jesus healed the physically blind, but as we know, there is not one so blind as he who cannot see. Spiritual blindness is much worse.

Years ago, a neighbor adamantly told me that Catholicism was the only way to heaven. I did not want to argue with her, but rather than identifying differences in our beliefs, I went for common ground, and tried to convince her that God had His hand on my life without my attendance at a Catholic church. I told her about the miracles He had accomplished in my life, the peace and joy He had given me. But she would not budge, in her own self-righteous bravado. Within the year, she left Catholicism and became a Hari Krishna. Someone who would abandon their beliefs that easily must not believe what they claim to believe.

Jesus healing the sick should have opened their eyes. Jesus fulfilling so many Old Testament prophecies should have convinced them. But the act of Jesus forgiving sins offended them. Even then, at the very least, they should have watched Him extra closely, to see if this could possibly be the Messiah that Scriptures had told them about. The darkness upon the earth during the daytime crucifixion of Jesus and the earthquake that split the Temple veil from top to bottom after the death of Jesus should have opened their eyes. "We have killed our Messiah!" But there is a difference between blindness and sheer refusal to open one's eyes.

Let's return to the authority of Jesus. We can see that authority, with Jesus teaching in the synagogue, soon after He called James and John as disciples:

> They were amazed at His teaching; for He was teaching them as *one* having authority, and not as the scribes.
> Mark 1:26 (NASB)

What was the comparison between the teaching of Jesus and the teaching of others? Authority! In Hebrew tradition, a rabbi took only a small number of students, and typically, looked for the most promising students. Paul, for example, studied under the leading rabbi, Gamaliel, a leader in the *Sanhedrin*. Yet, Jesus had not studied with a rabbi, and still spoke with more understanding and authority than any rabbi. This verse demonstrates to us that while the scribes and Pharisees would not acknowledge the authority of Jesus, regular people could "see that authority," without being experts! Again, the authority of Jesus came from God the Father, and as God the Son, the authority of Jesus was irrefutable. This was in direct conflict with the authority of the Jewish leadership, man-appointed and self-glorifying. Let's look at another aspect of the authority of Jesus:

> [31] And He came down to Capernaum, a city of Galilee, and He was teaching them on the Sabbath; [32] and they were amazed at His teaching, for His message was with authority. [33] In the synagogue there was a man possessed by the spirit of an unclean demon, and he cried out with a loud voice, [34] "Let us alone! What business do we have with each other, Jesus of Nazareth? Have You come to destroy us? I know who You are—the Holy One of God!" [35] But Jesus rebuked him, saying, "Be quiet and come out of him!" And when the demon had thrown him down in the midst *of the people*, he came out of him without doing him any harm. [36] And amazement came upon them all, and they began talking with one another saying, "What is this message? For with authority and power He commands the unclean spirits and they come out." [37] And the report about Him was spreading into every locality in the surrounding district.
> Luke 4:31-37 (NASB)

This is Luke's description of our previous story told by Mark. Notice that the word "authority" appears twice in this passage. The first use of the word in this passage speaks of the authority of Jesus teaching the Old Testament, but then, a commotion arises. Personally, I have experienced disruptive people in church services and Bible studies, but not as disruptive as a demon-possessed man. This demon not only acknowledged and identified Jesus as the Holy One of God, but then when Jesus commanded the demon to come out of the man, and not to harm the man, the demon obeyed. People not only saw this, but acknowledged the authority of Jesus. What happened to those people? How could their opened eyes have closed again? Are we as believers so unfocused that some of the truths we have learned about God are forgotten? Do we have eyes to see and ears to hear, then become blind and deaf once again?

85

There is no place in the Bible where the authority of Jesus is any more apparent than in His prayer in John 17. Though churches today repeat the Lord's Prayer of Matthew 6 frequently, the prayer of Jesus before enduring the cross demonstrates His love for us so succinctly. Personally, I am not big on repeating the prayers of others, even repeating the prayers of Jesus, as a prayer should come from my heart. In prayer, I can communicate my innermost thoughts and desires directly to the Creator of all. In the Lord's Prayer, Jesus answered the question of the disciples when asked how to pray. But in that prayer, Jesus did not answer, "What should be the exact wording of our prayers?" The Lord's Prayer includes important aspects of prayer, and for the Father's will to be done. But in His prayer in John 17, Jesus spent the first few verses praying for His own needs just before He endured the cross. Imagine what is about to occur, and rather than focusing lengthily on His own needs, Jesus focused the majority of His words on His followers. After praying for Himself, Jesus prayed for His disciples, and then, He prayed for all believers to come, us. Let's look specifically at His authority!

> [1] Jesus spoke these things; and lifting up His eyes to heaven, He said, "Father, the hour has come; glorify Your Son, that the Son may glorify You, [2] even as You gave Him authority over all flesh, that to all whom You have given Him, He may give eternal life. [3] "This is eternal life, that they may know You, the only true God, and Jesus Christ whom You have sent. [4] "I glorified You on the earth, having accomplished the work which You have given Me to do. [5] "Now, Father, glorify Me together with Yourself, with the glory which I had with You before the world was. [6] "I have manifested Your name to the men whom You gave Me out of the world; they were Yours and You gave them to Me, and they have kept Your word. [7] "Now they have come to know that everything You have given Me is from You;
> John 17:1-7 (NKJV)

That authority of Jesus, over all flesh, was God-given, Father-given. This should not be eye-opening or surprising, as it makes perfect sense that the Creator of all would also have authority over all. Has your mother ever stated, "I brought you into this world and I can take you out of it?" On this earth, God has given dominion to Satan for a time, and a battle is being waged. Yet we never should get discouraged by that battle. How is it possible for a created-being to defeat the One who created him? Think of an NBA team playing a team of 5-year-olds, yet the difference between those teams is not as great as the difference between God and Satan. If you are discouraged, read the end of God's book and the last chapter in Revelation. When the battle will end is something we do not know, but how it will end already is set in stone. Jesus departed the perfection of heaven to come to earth and do the will of the Father. We may think of being glorified as being high and lifted up, but the only way that occurred when Jesus came to earth was when He was high and lifted up on the cross! Through the authority of the Father, given to the Son, we as believers are given eternal life.

Our first step was to understand God's *agape* love. Next, keeping that love at the forefront of our minds and hearts, we learn to abide in that love, and abide in the Vine. Jesus is the Vine, and He gives us the strength to endure anything, and at the same time, He offers forgiveness when we fail. In some ways, it might seem easier to us if God chose to remove sin from us the moment we come to Him, yet instead, He has perfectly chosen to allow our struggle with sin to continue. In that process, we learn more about His love, through the grace of His forgiveness. In addition, we also learn that our behavior, or adherence to the Law, does not cause God to love us more. It is not possible for God to love us more; nor is it possible for us to earn His love. Instead, accept the gift! Unwrap it! Cherish it! That gift is grace – God's Riches At Christ's Expense – getting something we do not deserve. Through His grace, we are His for all eternity. Death will be a mere blink of the eye, and in that moment, we will journey from absent from the body to present with the Lord. So, our journey here is about abiding in Him.

Next, we addressed another important aspect of our lives with Him. "*Amen,*" reminds us to agree with the Father's will. I often have heard people pray this Psalm:

> Delight yourself also in the Lord,

And He shall give you the desires of your heart.
Psalm 37:4 (NKJV)

It is basically an if-then statement. If we delight ourselves in the Lord, then He will give us the desires of our hearts. This is a frequently misunderstood verse. What does it mean to delight ourselves in the Lord? What if we most desire a new Lamborghini? When we delight ourselves in the Lord, our hearts are aligned with God's heart. Consequently, what we want from God is what He desires to give us, as He is incapable of giving His children bad gifts. Sorry to take away your Lamborghini, but unless God has a purpose in you having a Lamborghini, my guess is the money used to buy such an expensive toy could bless others with more pressing needs. Jesus always prayed in the will of the Father, and we should also pray for the will of the Father and in the name of Jesus. When our hearts reflect the heart of God, and we are in complete agreement with Him, AMEN!

Finally, when Jesus uttered that statement twice at the beginning of a verse, "*Amen, Amen*," those verses should pique our interest that He is speaking in authority. When we accept the authority of God in our lives, and also on this broken world, we come to realize that worry is a waste. Be content in all things, knowing that God is in control of our lives. Through His authority, nothing can harm us. Certainly, nothing can separate us, either.

Alpha
Agape
Abide
Amen
Authority

These first two parts of this book are about our relationships with God, and in Part Three, we will now focus on our relationships with others. Once we are saved, there is a reason that God does not immediately take us to heaven. He keeps us here, and allows us to affect others. In addition to building His kingdom, God wants us to affect others, even those who never will choose Him.

Part Three:
Sharing God's Love
With Others

Chapter Five: The Greatest Commandment

What has changed so drastically in modern culture? Most are familiar with the adage that history repeats itself, or specifically, those who do not learn history are destined to repeat it. King Solomon said something similar, albeit years earlier:

> That which has been *is* what will be,
> That which is done *is* what will be done,
> And *there is* nothing new under the sun.
> Ecclesiastes 1:9 (NKJV)

But even with those words of wisdom, our collective belief in God has changed immensely. In the days of Noah, God destroyed His Creation, apart from a representation of all the animals He had created, and eight people. Certainly, at that time, people did not honor God. When we dig into the biblical passages concerning the ages of the first generations of mankind, we find that Lamech, the father of Noah, was 56-years-old when Adam died, nine generations later! At the time of the Great Flood, a man's father, one generation removed, could have known the first man (his relative), and could have known a man who walked and talked with God! That is very close to an eyewitness and visual evidence of God. Noah surely believed, otherwise, why would he hear a voice and spend 100 years of intense labor building an ark? And don't forget, when he began, Noah was 500-years-old, and Noah finished the ark 100 years later. God still speaks to His children today.

Throughout history, we can see world philosophy change, though, from monotheism to polytheism. Certainly, polytheism was pervasive in the Greek and Roman cultures, in addition to Israel's neighboring nations, as God warned His chosen people not to marry foreign wives. God knew exactly what would happen. The northern tribes of Israel fell into idolatry, worshipping false gods, as idolatry became a constant battle for Israel. But what is happening in modern culture takes this to a different level. About 7% of Americans identify as either atheist or agnostic. Certainly, there are many more who may believe in God, but do not believe He has anything to do with our lives. Most of this comes down to pride, as people desire to be the gods of their own lives. All we have to do is remember Adam, for just as Adam, we are all rule-breakers more than rule-followers. Regardless of man's desire not to honor God, God desires relationship with His creation, He created the Law to benefit man, and in so doing, began that process of giving man a way to know Him. In this passage, we know that the Jews did not see God, but they certainly heard Him, and that scared them:

> [23] "So it was, when you heard the voice from the midst of the darkness, while the mountain was burning with fire, that you came near to me, all the heads of your tribes and your elders. [24] And you said: 'Surely the Lord our God has shown us His glory and His greatness, and we have heard His voice from the midst of the fire. We have seen this day that God speaks with man; yet he *still* lives. [25] Now therefore, why should we die? For this great fire will consume us; if we hear the voice of the Lord our God anymore, then we shall die.

God did not design His Law to destroy man, but to make man whole and holy. Following the Law was an arduous process, but even to a non-believer, following the Law would be beneficial. That is why the battle in American courtrooms to remove the 10 Commandments is so ridiculous. What is offensive about, "Thou shalt not kill?" Only murderers would be offended. When Jesus came, He did a little addition by subtraction. First, Jesus wanted us to know that He did not come to do away with the Law:

> [16] "Let your light shine before men in such a way that they may see your good works, and glorify your Father who is in heaven. [17] "Do not think that I came to abolish the Law or the Prophets; I did not come to abolish but to fulfill. [18] "For truly I say to you, until heaven and earth pass away, not the smallest letter or stroke shall pass from the Law until all is accomplished.
> Matthew 5:16-18 (NASB)

The smallest letter and stroke identified in verse 18 are the *jot* and *tittle*. A *jot* is the smallest Hebrew letter, while the *tittle* is the dot above certain Hebrew letters. For example, here is the word *Elohim*, meaning God, plural (אֱלֹהִים). The letter that looks like an apostrophe is the *yud*, or *jot*, while the little dot above the middle letter is the *tittle*. Jesus made sure that we understood the Law remained intact. This makes perfect sense, for if God simply did away with the Law, and He is omniscient, it would make us question that omniscience, for why would God abolish what He already had created perfectly? In his letter to the Galatians, Paul explains the purpose of the Law:

> [24] Therefore the law was our tutor *to bring us* to Christ, that we might be justified by faith. [25] But after faith has come, we are no longer under a tutor.
> Galatians 3:24-25 (NKJV)

God's Law identifies sin. Many people today easily can see that a murderer or rapist is a sinner, but do not perceive themselves as sinners. Yet by simply reading the 10 Commandments, no man would doubt that he has fallen short and broken at least one of those commandments. The first four commandments deal with man's relationship with God, while the last six commandments deal with man's relationship with man. Then Jesus took it to a whole new level:

> [29] Jesus answered him, "The first of all the commandments is: *'Hear, O Israel, the Lord* our God, the Lord is one. [30] *And you shall* love the Lord your God with all your heart, with all your soul, with all your mind, and with all your strength.'* This is the first commandment. [31] And the second, like it, is this: *'You shall love your neighbor as yourself.'* There is no other commandment greater than these."
> Mark 12:29-31 (NKJV)

Jesus began by quoting the *Shema* (Deuteronomy 6:1), and after reminding us to love the Lord our God, the Lord my God, with all of our heart, soul, mind and strength, we should love our neighbor as much as we love ourselves. These commandments do not replace the 10 Commandments of the Old Testament, but they certainly summarize those commandments. If we love the Lord in the manner described, we will honor the first four commandments. If we love our neighbors in the manner described, we will honor the last six commandments. There is that *agape* love again. First, we must receive that *agape* love from the Lord, but next, we see what we are to do with it. Loving God is abiding in Him. Jesus reminded us that through our obedience, we demonstrate our love of God (John 14:15; John 14:23). Perhaps the most difficult challenge for us to obey God is to love others. In the remainder of this chapter, let's discuss loving other Christians, and then in the next chapter, emphasize loving non-believers.

Earlier in this book, we spent quite a bit of time looking more deeply at the passage in John 15 about abiding in the Vine. Interestingly, immediately after that passage, Jesus continued that thought with this one:

¹² This is My commandment, that you love one another as I have loved you. ¹³ Greater love has no one than this, than to lay down one's life for his friends. ¹⁴ You are My friends if you do whatever I command you. ¹⁵ No longer do I call you servants, for a servant does not know what his master is doing; but I have called you friends, for all things that I heard from My Father I have made known to you. ¹⁶ You did not choose Me, but I chose you and appointed you that you should go and bear fruit, and *that* your fruit should remain, that whatever you ask the Father in My name He may give you. ¹⁷ These things I command you, that you love one another.
John 15:12-17 (NKJV)

Jesus identified His friends as those who obey Him. Certainly, obedience to the Lord places us in an entirely different category. Abraham was called a friend of God in Isaiah 41:8 and James 2:23. In John 15, we see that Jesus considers obedient believers as His friends, too. I always have wondered if we as believers also can refer to God as our friend. Think of a powerful king who refers to a lowly man as his friend. At the same time, would the lowly man be able to make the same statement, or does the king's position make this different? I do not have an answer, but it seems to me that even though God calls us friends, we are attempting to bring Him down to our level when we refer to Him as friend, rather than worshipping Him as God! We need to retain reverence for God. In this verse, Jesus speaks of a different kind of love. This love is so great that a man will give up the most precious gift, his life, for his friends. Loving our neighbor as ourselves is quite different, indeed, for when we love someone just as we love ourselves, we are loving them exactly as much as we love ourselves. Instead, sacrificial love demonstrates that we love others more than we love ourselves! Otherwise, how could we emphasize their lives more than we emphasize our own?

Imagine a church body that loves each other in this manner. We actually can see this kind of love represented in the early church in the Book of Acts. Everyone collectively took care of the needs within the church. In Acts 5, though, we see an interesting situation where Ananias sold a possession, and claiming that he was giving all of the proceeds to the church, he held back part of the profits. Peter pointed out that there was no need for Ananias to lie, as there was no law that a man had to donate every penny to the church. With that lie to the Holy Spirit, though, within moments, both Ananias and his wife Sapphira were dead. Obviously, the foundation of the church was important to God, for that church demonstrated such a strong love for each other. All needs were met, from rich to poor, married to widows. There are so many verses in the Bible instructing us to care for widows and orphans.

Yet somehow, today's church has changed much from that early church. Most people tend to look at their finances as something they earned, or as a blessing God has given to them individually. One of my dearest friends is a doctor, and certainly, his salary is much higher than mine. His salary, however, does not cause him to pridefully look at his life as something he has earned. Instead, he realizes that God gave him intelligence, drive and opportunity, and through diligence, his salary is substantial. Instead of driving expensive cars and living an elevated lifestyle, though, he looks for needs he can fill in the lives of others. Isn't that much more representative of the early church than it is of our modern culture? I also remember another believer who sued his ex-father-in-law for millions of dollars, and spent so much money on himself. He drove a Maserati, a BMW and a Range Rover, while there were poor people in the same small congregation having difficulty getting transportation to work or church. While finances may be only a small part of how we love others, if we have a love of money, that love gets in the way of loving others. Jesus emphasized this when He said a man cannot serve two masters, and spoke specifically of the inability to serve God and *mamman* (Matthew 6:24). *Mamman*, not surprisingly, means "riches." The love of money is the root of all evil, according to 1 Timothy 6:10. Notice that money is not the root of all evil, but the love of money. We all have a love of money to differing degrees, and that is why this is such an important area to demonstrate our love for fellow believers.

It would make sense if loving other believers came naturally to us as Christians. After all, we have the most important aspect of our lives in common, a love for God. Yet most of us also would acknowledge that when we are hurt by a non-Christian, it does not hurt nearly as much as it does when we are hurt by a Christian brother or sister. We sometimes make the same incorrect assessment frequently done by non-Christians, that Christians should not make mistakes. Yet we all know the truth. Christians are not perfect, but instead, forgiven. Our walks with God are unique, and all of us are at different points on that path. Our biggest focus should be to offer others the same grace that God has offered us. Let's begin by addressing a verse that Christians and non-Christians both quote:

> [1] "Judge not, that you be not judged. [2] For with what judgment you judge, you will be judged; and with the measure you use, it will be measured back to you. [3] And why do you look at the speck in your brother's eye, but do not consider the plank in your own eye? [4] Or how can you say to your brother, 'Let me remove the speck from your eye'; and look, a plank is in your own eye? [5] Hypocrite! First remove the plank from your own eye, and then you will see clearly to remove the speck from your brother's eye.
> Matthew 7:1-5 (NKJV)

I guess when we get "board" with our own lives, we look at the lives of others, and judge! First of all, what does it mean to judge? If we think about a courtroom, the judge is the one passing sentence. In order to do this, a judge needs information and wisdom. An example of an earthly judge with wisdom was King Solomon in 1 Kings 3:16-28, when Solomon's decision was to split a baby in half! As two women claimed to be the baby's mother, by offering this solution, Solomon quickly identified the true mother of the baby. Without wisdom, a judge is nothing better than an arrogant dictator, enforcing laws without knowledge. In the statement of Jesus from the Sermon on the Mount, He emphasized that God will judge us with the same standard in which we judge others. It sounds like we should err on the side of grace when judging others. After all, we never have all the information, though God does. Regardless of our personal opinions, or even the amount of pain the sin of another has caused, if we focus on the fact that we are all sinners, grace is of the highest importance.

I try to equate judgment with condemnation, and as I certainly would not like a "death sentence" in my life, but would prefer another chance, I try not to condemn another. When I look back on the egregious mistakes of my life, I still am amazed that God was willing to forgive me. Having that weighty burden released from my shoulders made me a new man. Wouldn't it be appropriate for me to offer that same gift to others?

In the same chapter from the previous biblical quotation, directly from the mouth of Jesus, we see another passage that seems to create many arguments:

> [15] "Beware of false prophets, who come to you in sheep's clothing, but inwardly they are ravenous wolves. [16] You will know them by their fruits. Do men gather grapes from thorn-bushes or figs from thistles? [17] Even so, every good tree bears good fruit, but a bad tree bears bad fruit. [18] A good tree cannot bear bad fruit, nor *can* a bad tree bear good fruit. [19] Every tree that does not bear good fruit is cut down and thrown into the fire. [20] Therefore by their fruits you will know them.
> Matthew 7:15-20 (NKJV)

In this passage, Jesus warned us to protect the flock, the children of God, from false prophets. Jesus further emphasized that we can identify these false prophets by looking at the fruit in their lives. Many Christians take this to mean that we are called to be "fruit inspectors," always assessing the lives of fellow believers. I emphatically disagree! First of all, let's define "prophet." In the Old Testament, God gave us both prophets and priests. Priests spoke to God on behalf of men, while prophets spoke to men on behalf of God. Jesus is an example of both, in addition to His role of King. In fact, the three items placed in the ark of the covenant all pointed to these roles of Jesus. The tablets of the 10 Commandments pointed to the role of Jesus as King, as only a king can make laws. Aaron's budding rod pointed to the role of Jesus as priest. Remember, that rod was a dead branch that came back to life to bear fruit. It was not the death of Jesus that enabled us to bear fruit, but His resurrection. And now, Jesus sits at God's right hand as our High Priest forever, according to Hebrews. Finally, the jar of *manna* points to the role of Jesus as prophet. He came as the true Bread of heaven, to speak to man for God! Jesus never misrepresented God, and at the same time, always represented the heart of the Father. So remember, if a prophet speaks to man for God, then a false prophet speaks to man, but does not speak for God. This could include false words, incorrect interpretations of the Bible, claiming to hear from God when they are instead speaking their own opinions, or even false predictions. If we think their words might be false, we likely will be able to see the lack of the fruit of the Spirit in their lives.

Let's look at an Old Testament statement concerning false prophets:

> [6] "If your brother, the son of your mother, your son or your daughter, the wife of your bosom, or your friend who is as your own soul, secretly entices you, saying, 'Let us go and serve other gods,' which you have not known, neither you nor your fathers, [7] of the gods of the people which *are* all around you, near to you or far off from you, from *one* end of the earth to the *other* end of the earth, [8] you shall not consent to him or listen to him, nor shall your eye pity him, nor shall you spare him or conceal him; [9] but you shall surely kill him; your hand shall be first against him to put him to death, and afterward the hand of all the people. [10] And you shall stone him with stones until he dies, because he sought to entice you away from the Lord your God, who brought you out of the land of Egypt, from the house of bondage. [11] So all Israel shall hear and fear, and not again do such wickedness as this among you.
> Deuteronomy 13:6-11 (NKJV)

Again, a prophet speaks to man for God, so a false prophet claims to correctly state the words of God, but does not. If his words are false, his relationship with God is equally false. A true prophet leads people to God. A false prophet leads people away from God, and God's encouragement to the nation of Israel was to put anyone to death who led believers to follow other gods. This may seem harsh, especially if that person was a sibling, but God wants us to know that our relationship with Him is paramount. Nothing is more important. Prophecy falls into two categories: speaking forth the Word of God and speaking of an event before it occurs, predicting with the knowledge given by God. Basically, prophecy can be forthtelling and foretelling. As I write this book, I am speaking out the Word of God. We also have seen many "date-setters," incorrectly giving us the day of God's rapture of the church, even though the Bible tells us that no one knows the hour or day of the return of Jesus. If a prophecy does not coincide with what it says in the Bible, it is false!

> [19] And so we have the prophetic word confirmed, which you do well to heed as a light that shines in a dark place, until the day dawns and the morning star rises in your hearts; [20] knowing this first, that no prophecy of Scripture is of any private interpretation, [21] for prophecy never came by the will of man, but holy men of God spoke *as they were* moved by the Holy Spirit.
> 2 Peter 1:19-21 (NKJV)

For those who believe that our roles of "fruit inspectors" apply to other believers with sin in their lives, remember that the cited passage is referring to false prophets, not struggling believers. If we know the words of the Bible, and we hear someone leading us astray, then we are to look at the fruit of their lives. What is fruit? Well, as discussed earlier, Galatians 5 identifies a whole list for us: love, joy, peace, longsuffering, kindness, goodness, faithfulness, gentleness and self-control. We also see another list there of aspects of lives that reveal the opposite of the fruit of the Spirit: adultery, fornication, uncleanness, lewdness, idolatry, sorcery, hatred, contentions, jealousies, outbursts of wrath, selfish ambitions, dissensions, heresies, envy, murders, drunkenness and revelries. Why are we to look at the fruit in the life of someone we suspect to be a false prophet? To me, at least part of this has to do with the fact that even as believers, we are all still sinners, lacking God's omniscience. Take for example this subject on being a "fruit inspector." If my opinion differs from yours, does it make either of us a false prophet for believing differently? As believers, we certainly have different opinions, yet we should err on the side of God's love, correctly representing who He tells us He is in His Word, rather than our own judgmental nature. But God wants us to spend time learning about Him, not waste time accusing and convicting another struggling with sin. After all, every believer continues to struggle with sin! Are we incorrectly convinced that their sin stinks more than our own?

If I went to an apple farm, I could tell you what apples were the prettiest on the outside, but without taking a bite of that apple, I would have no idea of the sweetness of its taste. But God knows the actions and also, knows the hearts and motives, of each person, just as He knows the sweetness of an apple without taking a bite. The earlier quotation from Matthew 7 emphasizes that we should be cautious looking at the tiny sins in the lives of others when we have large sins in our own lives. This encourages me not to judge others, as I know that my sins are many. Again, judgment is passing sentence. Isn't it wonderful that our journey continues and our whole story has not yet been written? God promises that He will complete His work in us, but that promise did not include God flipping a light switch, making each of us perfect the moment we asked Jesus into our lives. Err on the side of grace! As I desperately desire God's grace for my sin, should I not be willing to offer that grace to another believer?

This phrase of "fruit inspectors" seems to be catchy to many Bible teachers, but remember the specifics of the passage remind us to look at the fruit of the lives of those we suspect to be false prophets, not believers who have sinned. Without identifying the man's name, let me give an example. There is a best-seller "Christian" book teaching that everyone will go to heaven, and the author states repeatedly that there is no such place as hell. Is this man correctly teaching the words of the Bible? After all, Jesus taught often about hell. Was Jesus lying? If a man claims truth in a doctrine that contradicts the words of the Bible, and does so claiming to have a direct revelation from God, he is a false prophet. If this teaching leads people away from God, rather than leading people to God, what are we to do?

> [17] Now I urge you, brethren, note those who cause divisions and offenses, contrary to the doctrine which you learned, and avoid them. [18] For those who are such do not serve our Lord Jesus Christ, but their own belly, and by smooth words and flattering speech deceive the hearts of the simple. [19] For your obedience has become known to all. Therefore I am glad on your behalf; but I want you to be wise in what is good, and simple concerning evil. [20] And the God of peace will crush Satan under your feet shortly.
> The grace of our Lord Jesus Christ *be* with you. Amen.
> Romans 16:17-20 (NKJV)

Is the person I mentioned earlier, who teaches that hell does not exist, a Christian? Frankly, that is not up to me to decide. Hopefully, all believers continue to learn. When I look back at my first book written 10 years ago, I can see many statements that I made that I would not agree with completely now. My heart was right, though. With 10 additional years in God's Word, God continues to teach me. But even if I incorrectly stated something 10 years ago, does it mean I was not a believer? Absolutely not!

But I still pray that if I mis-stated anything in my books that God will have people gloss over that part when reading. I also go into this book prayerfully and with the heart that I will represent correctly God and God's Word. Hopefully, all believers are continuing to grow closer to the Lord, and to know more about Him through His Word. At the same time, Paul prods us to avoid those who are teaching in ways that cause division. In the passage from Romans cited above, we can identify those people as they, "do not serve our Lord Jesus Christ, but their own belly, and by smooth words and flattering speech deceive the hearts of the simple." If someone is using the Gospel to make lots of money, looking for a new doctrine, don't let that person deceive you. My goal in writing books has nothing to do with money. Instead, my prayer is that if each book written can bless even one person, it is worth the effort of writing.

I have given out more books than I have sold, but it is my ministry, and what I feel the Lord has called me to do. When judging others, be very cautious.

I remember a story about Pastor Chuck Smith, who started Calvary Chapel. One of his elders had left his wife of many years and moved in with a younger woman. Chuck went to the house where his elder was staying, went in, sat on the couch and wept. He never said a word. Chuck left and the next week, the elder was back at church and also returned to his wife. It did not take any judgment or condemnation, just heart!

Part of loving our fellow believers is to be willing to address difficult situations. If I see a believer struggling in sin, is it more helpful to ignore that sin, or to come alongside them and offer support? Often, God uses the sins in our pasts to encourage others walking a similar path through the amazing gift of empathy, or compassion. One of the most special times in my life was a year and a half when I was teaching a Bible study to three young men living in a sober-living home. All three had different drug-related issues, and all three were in different places in their recovery, mentally and physically. One was much farther along than the others, in my estimation, as he had handed it all over to Jesus. A second believed in God but honestly stated that he did not want God to control his life. The third had grown up in the church and was filled with head knowledge, but severely lacking in heart knowledge. At the same time, he was filled with animosity for others – homosexuals, for example – as he viewed their sin as much greater than his. He also had racist tendencies. Needless to say, all three presented different challenges for me. Typically, God uses people who have walked similar paths, but I never had stumbled with drugs, or even tried them. But as I taught Bible studies to these three young men, I reminded them that I had a sin addiction. My choice of sin might have been different than their choice of sin, but it was just as disgusting. My sin had broken me. I emphasized what we had in common, rather than what was different. Most importantly, I did what God had created me to do. I taught them His Word. Amazingly, eight years down the road, all three remain clean and sober. Two are now married with children and the other returned and earned his college degree. Our lives always will be tied together from that time that God placed us in each other's lives. Discipleship is more than just teaching the Word of God. Instead, it involves walking together, just as Jesus walked with the 12 for three years. In that time, we can encourage and admonish.

Addressing sin in a fellow believer must be edifying, not condemning. To edify is to build up, not tear down. Sometimes, it can be extremely difficult to not bring our own judgments to the table, but with love as our focus (there is that *agape* term again, reminding us how unconditionally God loves us), we can encourage them. We also need to understand the difference between encouragement and admonishment, as the Bible encourages us to do both! Admonishment is teaching while correcting. Here is a wonderful example of admonishment in the Bible:

> [24] Now a certain Jew named Apollos, born at Alexandria, an eloquent man *and* mighty in the Scriptures, came to Ephesus. [25] This man had been instructed in the way of the Lord; and being fervent in spirit, he spoke and taught accurately the things of the Lord, though he knew only the baptism of John. [26] So he began to speak boldly in the synagogue. When Aquila and Priscilla heard him, they took him aside and explained to him the way of God more accurately. [27] And when he desired to cross to Achaia, the brethren wrote, exhorting the disciples to receive him; and when he arrived, he greatly helped those who had believed through grace; [28] for he vigorously refuted the Jews publicly, showing from the Scriptures that Jesus is the Christ.
> Acts 18:24-28 (NKJV)

Apollos was not wrong, as he had been instructed in the ways of the Lord, and we also see that he was "fervent in the Spirit." Additionally, Apollos was mighty in the Scriptures. Keep in mind that the only written word at the time was the Old Testament. Apollos was a Jew, a follower of Jesus and an eloquent preacher. But Aquila and Priscilla knew something Apollos did not know. Notice that they did not question Apollos in public. Nor did they condemn him for his beliefs. Instead, they took him aside, privately, and instructed Apollos by explaining to him the baptism of the Holy Spirit. Who benefited from this event? Everyone! Certainly, it was a blessing to both Aquila and Priscilla to share these powerful words with a fellow believer, and then see those words affect his life. Also, it was beneficial to Apollos, as the Holy Spirit would change his life, too. Finally, it was a benefit to anyone to hear Apollos speak afterward. Sometimes, though, it can be difficult to admonish a fellow believer. This can have to do with how we deliver the message, but also can be affected by how the other person receives the message.

Though the Bible encourages us to be like the Bereans, searching the Scriptures daily to ensure that what we are learning is accurate (Acts 17:11), many pastors do not like to be questioned. Pride affects all men, and though we tend to put pastors on pedestals, pastors are just as likely to experience pride as other believers. Perhaps we add to that pride by placing them on pedestals. Logically, it is much simpler to admonish someone who is stationed below us. Think of a father admonishing a son. It is a little more tenuous for a son to admonish a father, though. Yet as believers, we are all parts of the same body. Just as Paul reminded us, an eye is not more important than a toe, and in the same manner, a pastor is not more important than the servant who cleans the restrooms. If God has given the gift, then operating in God's gift is perfect, if that is what the Lord intended. If a pastor is teaching something that does not agree with God's Word, it might take a little courage to have a private conversation. But through that courage, many people might be blessed. Again, though people may have looked at Apollos as the leader, due to his public role, Priscilla and Aquila still admonished him. There are at least two lessons here: one is to be willing to speak truth into people's lives and the other is to remain humble when someone speaks truth into your life!

I remember a situation where a pastor was teaching about Jesus as the Good Shepherd. He stated that if sheep continued to stray, the shepherd would break the legs of the sheep and carry the sheep. He also added that as pastor, he was called to break some legs. He did not get that concept from the Bible. In fact, this is one of those often-repeated stories that many pastors have used as an example, though for it to be a good example, it should at least reflect the words of the Bible. One particular woman in the church was completely offended by that statement. She pointed out that this story had no biblical basis. Realistically, doesn't it sound completely unlikely that a shepherd would risk the life of a sheep by breaking its legs, if the shepherd loved the sheep? Sheep, adult ewes in particular, weigh between 160 and 180 pounds when fully grown. Does the story sound legitimate? What if two sheep decided to stray? Is the shepherd going to carry both of them? I don't know many men capable of carrying 350 pounds as they walk through the hills. What sounds more likely with a legitimate shepherd is if a sheep strayed so much that it became problematic for the shepherd, that sheep would be the first choice for dinner! But Jesus, as the Good Shepherd, does not eat His sheep. This analogy also depicts Jesus as punitive, when that similarly contradicts the words of the Bible. Again, God chastens His children…builds them up, edifies them and sometimes we might find ourselves in difficult places caused by our bad decisions. There will come a time when Jesus will judge the world. We also know that God is slow to anger, and in the yet-unfulfilled judgments of Revelation, God will pour out His wrath on a sinful earth. Yet even then, God's wrath does not conflict His love. Jesus is the Good Shepherd, not a super-charged Tanya Harding! Sadly, though the woman approached the pastor with a loving heart, he was unwilling to either support his statement scripturally, or respond with humility. It was not the first time that he was unapproachable, and the congregation began to dwindle. Even when it is difficult, we are to admonish one another.

This has to do with accountability. As believers, one of the greatest gifts while on this earth is to have a fellow believer that we trust deeply. Through that trust, we can share details of our lives, and some of those details carry the weight of shame. But through our transparency, and the willingness of a brother or sister in the Lord to hold us accountable, admonishment happens almost naturally. In this process, we can see the body of Christ edified. Paul was a master of admonishment. Read Paul's epistles and it is obvious that one of the most important aspects was to address sin within the churches. Paul had this to say about admonishment:

> Now I myself am confident concerning you, my brethren, that you also are full of goodness, filled with all knowledge, able also to admonish one another.
> Romans 15:14 (NKJV)

Here is another example, differentiating between admonishing and making a fellow believer an enemy. After all, as believers, we are parts of the same body of Christ!

> [13] But *as for* you, brethren, do not grow weary *in* doing good. [14] And if anyone does not obey our word in this epistle, note that person and do not keep company with him, that he may be ashamed. [15] Yet do not count *him* as an enemy, but admonish *him* as a brother.
> 2 Thessalonians 3:13-15 (NKJV)

In the letters by Jesus to seven churches in the first three chapters of Revelation, only two of the letters did not contain a commendation (Sardis and Laodicea). Two of the letters (to Philadelphia and Smyrna) had no criticism. But with the other letters, Jesus both encouraged and admonished each church. It seems that the two often should go hand-in-hand, for while encouragement pushes us forward, admonishment gives us something to work on, and at the same time keeps us from allowing pride to get in the way. Paul encourages believers to finish the race strongly, and for most of us, that race is a marathon. Long races require much endurance, and much pain. What helps us to finish the race is the knowledge that there is something to be gained by finishing. First of all, the pain will be gone, but there is that goal of a prize. For believers, we are going to a place where there will be no pain, no suffering, no sin and no tears, and whether or not there is a crown waiting for us, our prize is Jesus for all of eternity. It is certainly worth running the race! Additionally, though, we should have the hearts of picking up others around us who are struggling to continue the race.

Every believer needs encouragement, at one time or another. God has a ministry for every believer, and He gives us at least one spiritual gift. All it takes is a word from one blessed by our ministry to encourage us with God's purpose and plan. Encouraging and loving others are perfect examples of sharing our *agape* love with fellow believers. Even though I am singling out those gifts, every spiritual gift from God is an example of *agape* love when shared selflessly with others. Let's look at the different Bible passages concerning these spiritual gifts:

> [6] Since we have gifts that differ according to the grace given to us, *each of us is to exercise them accordingly*: if prophecy, according to the proportion of his faith; [7] if service, in his serving; or he who teaches, in his teaching; [8] or he who exhorts, in his exhortation; he who gives, with liberality; he who leads, with diligence; he who shows mercy, with cheerfulness.
> Romans 12:6-8 (NASB)

> [4] Now there are varieties of gifts, but the same Spirit. [5] And there are varieties of ministries, and the same Lord. [6] There are varieties of effects, but the same God who works all things in all *persons*. [7] But to each one is given the manifestation of the Spirit for the common good. [8] For to one is given the word of wisdom through the Spirit, and to another the word of knowledge according to the same Spirit; [9] to another faith by the same Spirit, and to another gifts of healing by the one Spirit, [10] and to another the effecting of miracles, and to another prophecy, and to another the distinguishing of spirits, to another *various* kinds of tongues, and to another the interpretation of tongues. [11] But one and the same Spirit works all these things, distributing to each one individually just as He wills.
> 1 Corinthians 12:4-11 (NASB)

> And God has appointed in the church, first apostles, second prophets, third teachers, then miracles, then gifts of healings, helps, administrations, *various* kinds of tongues.

Remember, there are no small gifts. For years, I claimed to be an atheist, which actually is quite laughable when I think back on it. Having made some horrendous life decisions, I was broken and alone. And claiming to be an atheist, one day I looked up into the sky and told God that I hated Him! Imagine how ludicrous it is to hate someone who does not exist. Logically, I must have believed in God to be angry at Him and to blame Him for my difficulties. Even as believers, though, we often take credit when life is going smoothly, and blame God when it is not. Most of our suffering comes from our own bad choices. With hindsight, I can certainly see that in my life. While I was walking in sin, doing what was right in my own eyes and claiming to be an atheist, my sister Julee had an all-night prayer meeting in her college dorm, where they focused on my salvation. People I never had met loved me so much that they gave up a sleepless night in college for me. Years later, that same sister got married, and she had two different, wedding events in locations that were not near each other. I had rented a car, and offered a ride to one of Julee's friends in attendance at the wedding. The day before, I stopped at a store and purchased a few Christian worship CDs, and was playing them that day, singing along and praising the Lord while driving through the backwoods of Virginia. In the backseat, I saw Julee's friend sobbing. I asked her why and she told me about the prayer meeting years before, and that Julee had not shared with her that I had come to the Lord. When I shared my testimony, the sobbing continued, and increased, because I was crying with her. How humbling it is to feel that kind of love from someone you do not even know! But God knew us both, and used her in my life. How could this be explained without understanding God's *agape* love, the same love He has His children share with others? How should that event change me? Well, certainly, knowing how deeply that love affected me, how can I affect someone else just as deeply? Pass it on, and continue to pass it on!

One of my favorite Bible teachers frequently opened by asking those in attendance to raise their hands if they were in ministry. The first time, I remember looking around to see how many people there who were pastors. But then the teacher reminded us that if we are following Jesus, we are all in ministry, and then he asked the question again. Of course, all hands were raised. This year, Billy Graham died, and living in Charlotte at the time, I spent many hours reflecting on how many lives he had touched with his ministry. Not to negate in any way what Billy Graham did, but he would be the last one to toot his own horn. If God's purpose in your life is to touch one specific person with God's love, and you follow through, you have accomplished your ministry. The ministry that God gave to Billy Graham might have been more public, but when we are operating in the ministry God has for us, we feel His pleasure! Do you have any idea how much joy I have writing this book? For years, I was an empty vessel with God as my enemy, and now He allows me to write about Him. Praise Him! I am eternally grateful!

After telling the story of lost sheep, the lost Prodigal son and lost coins, Jesus made this statement:

> "In the same way, I tell you, there is joy in the presence of the angels of God over one sinner who repents."
> Luke 15:10 (NASB)

Think about that for a moment. Angels celebrated when each of us came to the Lord. I have felt this same joy watching a new believer getting baptized. It does not matter if I ever have met them, tears always stream down my cheeks. Just like the angels, I am celebrating a new addition to our body! If only we kept that same focus through church splits, hurt feelings and jealousies. Sometimes, it is difficult to understand why believers don't all get along. After all, if God chose us, and He is incapable of making a mistake, why can't we love someone whom God loves? It seems like a natural progression, but all of us have experienced situations where our feelings get hurt by a fellow believer. Instead of thinking of all believers as family, notice that God gave us the analogy of the body, instead. While we see arguments within our families, when is the last time you can think of one of your body parts arguing against another body part? If I pull my left hamstring, my right hamstring and other muscles must do extra work just for me to walk. Should I expect my right hamstring to refuse to talk to my left hamstring, in anger for its added work? Should the right hamstring hold the left hamstring accountable, and ask for a vacation next week to make up for that extra work done this week? I might add that the left hamstring never apologized, even though it wasn't the left hamstring's idea to become injured. This might sound silly, but people, even fellow believers, would fail in exactly that manner. Is that why God described us as the "body of Christ" instead of the "family of Christ?" Certainly, there are battles in every family. God has been working on me this year involving one of those. Even as I write about God's *agape* love, when I looked inside, I could see a family member that I was struggling to love. One of the best blessings of this year is my realization that sometimes, no matter what we do, we cannot have peace with all men, but nothing can stop us from prayer. Nothing can stop us from loving from afar, hoping the best.

God wants us to get along. He also wants us to remember the sins He has forgiven in our lives. Remembering those sins will give us compassion when dealing with others, and yes, this includes those we feel have sinned against us. In all actuality, no sin is truly against us. All sin is against God, and if God can forgive, why can't we? I have pointed out to others that I know something God doesn't know, even though He is omniscient! I know my sin, but God has chosen to forget it. He does not want my sin to depress me, defeat me or destroy me, but God does want me to remember it. In so doing, I also will remember His forgiveness. At the same time, I will remember the feeling of that great burden being lifted off of my shoulders and placed on the shoulders of my Savior, Jesus. Knowing the freedom I felt from His removal of my sin, wouldn't I want others to feel that, as well? How can they, when I continue to carry a grudge, or worse, hate someone else? There is no excuse for that in the life of a believer.

Other than forgiveness, the greatest gift we have to share with another believer is time. One church I attended tried to start its own Bible college, and four of us taught one Saturday a month for a couple years on various subjects. One of the teachers made a deep impact on me when he offered this nugget, "Tithe your time." This does not mean that we should not support God's ministries financially, but think of the value of time. With 16 or so hours that I am awake each day, if I tithe my time, I will give the Lord 1.6 hours a day. If I base my tithe on 24 hours, the time tithe is 2.4 hours. When writing the devotional, I spent about 4 hours a day researching, studying, praying and writing, and looking back on it, that was one of the most special years of my life. This year, I signed up for an intense study of Romans through Bible Study Fellowship, and the daily homework was at least an hour and a half. And again, this has been an amazing year. Part of that time tithe should be personal time spent with the Lord. I think of the biblical story of Jesus in the home of Mary and Martha:

> [38] Now as they were traveling along, He entered a village; and a woman named Martha welcomed Him into her home. [39] She had a sister called Mary, who was seated at the Lord's feet, listening to His word.[40] But Martha was distracted with all her preparations; and she came up *to Him* and said, "Lord, do You not care that my sister has left me to do all the serving alone? Then tell her to help me." [41] But the Lord answered and said to her, "Martha, Martha, you are worried and bothered about so many things; [42] but *only* one thing is necessary, for Mary has chosen the good part, which shall not be taken away from her."
> Luke 10:38-42 (NASB)

I remember seeing a book entitled, "Being Mary in a Martha World," and it made me smile. Certainly, there is a balance. Each year, I do a Christian *Seder*, a Jewish feast of Moses commemorating Passover. I cook the food, serve the food, play the worship music and lead the *Seder*. Honestly, it is an intensely busy night, with over a month of preparation. The hardest part for me is the music, as I am not a naturally-gifted musician, either with guitar or singing. I get by, though. This year, I remember thinking that it didn't really matter how much time and energy I put into the *Seder*, if it allowed other people to sit at the feet of Jesus and worship, it was certainly worth-while. Martha's issue, in the story above, is that she was not willing to give Mary a chance to sit at the Savior's feet. However, we need

112

to make sure that we are not always requiring someone else do to the work while we sit and worship the Lord. Give them a chance, too. Yet even when we are working for the Lord, we still can be worshipping Him. There's a wonderful book written in the 1600s by Brother Lawrence called, "The Practice of the Presence of God," which gives amazing examples and encouragement to praise the Lord in the midst of the most menial tasks.

If we are spending time fellowshipping with the Lord, worshiping Him and learning His Word, we also need to spend time in ministry, serving others. One of the greatest ways to serve others as believers is discipleship. All believers should be involved in this! Jesus said:

> [19] "Go therefore and make disciples of all the nations, baptizing them in the name of the Father and the Son and the Holy Spirit, [20] teaching them to observe all that I commanded you; and lo, I am with you always, even to the end of the age."
> Matthew 28:19-20 (NASB)

Many people have made the excuse that they do not have the gift of teaching. Think about a 6-year-old boy teaching a 5-year-old boy to tie his shoes. We do not have to know everything to be a teacher. In fact, no teacher does know everything. Instead, we are called by the Lord to give out what He has given us. One of the most important aspects of teaching is the personal application. Paul described a "thorn in his flesh" in 2 Corinthians 12. One of the many reasons that thorn was not specifically identified could be that all of us can wonder if Paul stuggled with the same struggles we are facing. When teaching another person about the continued struggles when we are believers, I can share with them my struggles. The struggles before I walked with Jesus had no solution, but because of Jesus, He is my solution to any issue I may be facing now. Again, this is the living and breathing Word of God that has one interpretation, but many applications. Applications can be unique and very personal, and at the same time, can have a corporate application, applying to a specific group, and even to the entire body of Christ. Most importantly, this goes back to time.

Time spent with another person makes the greatest impact. One example that comes to mind has to do with one of my best friends, who has supported me through every hardship I have had as a believer. Recently, he has been enduring some difficult decisions for a relative with declining health. In one phone conversation, he was a little short with me. The next day he called to apologize, and I told him that no apology was necessary. I know his heart. We have spent so much time together, especially time in God's Word, that I realize that any infraction is temporary. Peter used different words to sum this up:

> And above all things have fervent love for one another, for *"love will cover a multitude of sins."*
> 1 Peter 4:8 (NKJV)

When someone loves us (there is that *agape* word again), that carries us through any disagreement, for we know that our love for the Lord and our love for each other can endure all things. Sometimes, we think that the mess in our lives becomes almost unbearable. But by serving others, we start seeing the difficulties in the lives of others, and that becomes our focus. What is our model for discipleship? Jesus! Nothing needs to be added to that statement. When we are discipling another, we are sharing God's truths with them, walking with them, knowing them and loving them. Transparency brings us closer. In a recent Bible study, we discussed the fact that most men do not have any close friends, other than their wives. But sometimes, we need another man to confide in, to discuss our deepest thoughts and ideas. We also need the safety of sharing those feelings without worrying that anyone else is going to hear what we shared in confidence and betray us. People should have confidence in your confidence! At one time in my Christian walk, because we have personal relationships with Jesus, I felt like I did not need those close friendships. While many answers are in the Bible, there are some decisions that we will not find an outright answer, biblically. Should I stay in California or move to North Carolina? Well, in Psalms it says to move! (Not really, that was just an example). But discussing those decisions with godly friends, who you have grown to trust, and to pray with them when we just do not know what direction to take, is part of discipleship. It does not really matter if you are the one discipling or being discipled, it is a two-way street. Both are blessed! If you don't know where to start, if you are a new believer, find a more mature believer you trust and ask them to disciple you. If you are a mature believer, find a new believer and offer to disciple them. If you are sharing the Lord with others, you might be the one who sees that planted seed come to fruition when that person accepts the Lord. That is a perfect time to offer discipleship. Though this book is not quite one-on-one, it certainly is my attempt at discipleship, trying to impart some of the wisdom God has given me.

Rusty Foster made the biggest impact on me as a new believer, and discipled me, years ago. He had been a missionary for 40+ years. At one time, I rented a room from Rusty, and we spent countless hours discussing the Bible. I remember one Christmas Eve, sitting at the table with Rusty and his wife, and Rusty's daughter and son-in-law. Rusty and I talked Bible for at least four hours that night, maybe the most memorable Christmas of my life. His specialty was the Book of Hebrews. One night, I was giving my first sermon at a rescue mission. I came out of there so pumped up, so excited that God had opened a door for me to teach the Word. Rusty came to support me. On the way out, I turned right to my car and Rusty turned left, sat down with a drunken homeless man, and began sharing Jesus with him. I turned around to see where Rusty was and started crying. For I realized that I had been so prideful in God using me that I had missed the humble opportunity to share His Word with a man who needed Jesus desperately. Rusty is now with the Lord. Every time I parted his company, Rusty said, "Here, there or in the air," referring to seeing each other again. I am guessing it is going to be there, in heaven!

Just last week, I spoke with Matt, one of the young men I discipled, and congratulated him on his 8-year anniversary of sobriety. We still can spend hours talking about Jesus on the phone. Matt has a heavenly father, and a really great earthly father, too, but in many ways, he always will be my spiritual son. But while I was teaching him, he was a challenge! Maybe that is the way it is supposed to be, for it only brought us closer. "Disciple" means learner, but there is an additional aspect of follower.

> [31] So Jesus was saying to those Jews who had believed Him, "If you continue in My word, *then* you are truly disciples of Mine; [32] and you will know the truth, and the truth will make you free."
> John 8:31-32 (NASB)

I am a disciple of Jesus, and I follow Him – His words and His deeds. Paul made a statement in 1 Corinthians 4:16 where he said, "Imitate me." The first time I read that, I thought it was rather arrogant, but as I have grown as a believer, there are men in my life who I imitate. Their love has changed me, as I see how they love others, forgive others and see that everyone is redeemable. If we are following close behind Jesus, not straying from His path, then someone right behind us is going in exactly the same direction. That is what discipleship is all about!

Addressing open sin is another difficult subject. Paul explains this process eloquently in 1 Corinthians 5, beginning by acknowledging that he is aware that a believer in the church of Corinth was in a sexual relationship with his own father's wife (or ex-wife). The Old Testament explained why this behavior was unacceptable, stating that it was uncovering one's father. (See Deuteronomy 22). In fact, the oldest son of Jacob, Reuben, lost his birthright by doing the same. Let's look at Paul's words concerning how the church is to handle this kind of sin:

> [1] It is actually reported *that there is* sexual immorality among you, and such sexual immorality as is not even named among the Gentiles—that a man has his father's wife! [2] And you are puffed up, and have not rather mourned, that he who has done this deed might be taken away from among you. [3] For I indeed, as absent in body but present in spirit, have already judged (as though I were present) him who has so done this deed. [4] In the name of our Lord Jesus Christ, when you are gathered together, along with my spirit, with the power of our Lord Jesus Christ, [5] deliver such a one to Satan for the

destruction of the flesh, that his spirit may be saved in the day of the Lord Jesus.

⁶ Your glorying is not good. Do you not know that a little leaven leavens the whole lump? ⁷ Therefore purge out the old leaven, that you may be a new lump, since you truly are unleavened. For indeed Christ, our Passover, was sacrificed for us. ⁸ Therefore let us keep the feast, not with old leaven, nor with the leaven of malice and wickedness, but with the unleavened *bread* of sincerity and truth.

1 Corinthians 5:1-8 (NKJV)

In verse five, Paul admonishes the Church of Corinth to deliver this man to Satan. That sounds harsh, doesn't it? When we think of the heart or the motive, though, it is edifying. By handing a believer over to Satan, that Satan may have his way with the man, that man will become broken and will walk away from his sin, sooner or later. What is worse, brokenness that comes from our sin or eternal damnation? God's heart is that we are all saved. Yet in a church body, unaddressed sin will create more sin. Have you ever attended a church service where the pastor spoke strongly against homosexuality, but failed to address the heterosexual unmarried couples living together and sleeping together within his church body? Any sexual relations outside of marriage is sin, sexual immorality, and we don't have the right to rank those sins. If we allow open sin in the midst of the church, one lump of leaven will leaven the whole lump. If you need a more updated way of looking at that concept, one bad apple will spoil the whole bunch. Interestingly, in the subsequent verses in 1 Corinthians 5, Paul goes on to differentiate between believers and non-believers:

⁹ I wrote to you in my epistle not to keep company with sexually immoral people. ¹⁰ Yet *I* certainly *did* not *mean* with the sexually immoral people of this world, or with the covetous, or extortioners, or idolaters, since then you would need to go out of the world. ¹¹ But now I have written to you not to keep company with anyone named a brother, who is sexually immoral, or covetous, or an idolater, or a reviler, or a drunkard, or an extortioner—not even to eat with such a

117

person.[12] For what *have* I *to do* with judging those also who are outside? Do you not judge those who are inside? [13] But those who are outside God judges. Therefore *"put away from yourselves the evil person."*
1 Corinthians 5:9-13 (NKJV)

What if we have an unmarried couple attending our church? Do we immediately throw them out of the church as soon as they accept the Lord? Personally, this decision must be "grace-based," as God does not flip a switch to cut all sin out of our lives. If that couple continues to fellowship in the church, God will open doors with the perfect time to speak truth to them. Either they need to get married, or stop sleeping together. But for a brand-new believer, encourage rather than condemn. If that same couple is attending your church but has not committed to Jesus, there is no reason to bring that subject up, unless they ask. This does not only apply to sexual sin. What if a drunken man stumbles into your church, desperately needing to hear from God? Should we toss him out? Before people have accepted Jesus, they are slaves to sin, and sin is as natural as breathing. If we condemn sinners, and will not speak to them, who will share Jesus with them? What if a believer admits to hating homosexuals? As believers, do we have the right to hate anyone? Is their sin worse than my sin in the eyes of God, yet He still loves me and forgave me? Every one of us has people who are difficult to love in our lives. But again, whether to love or not to love is not our option. It is simple to love those who love us, and quite more complicated to love the unlovable. But it is the unlovable who need love the most. The need for God's love is the greatest, but our love may lead them there.

In Matthew 18, Jesus gave instructions to Peter concerning how to address sin between brothers. Remember, all sin is against God, though we pridefully can become offended when someone infringes on what we see as our rights.

[15] "Moreover if your brother sins against you, go and tell him his fault between you and him alone. If he hears you, you have gained your brother. [16] But if he will not hear, take with

118

you one or two more, that *'by the mouth of two or three witnesses every word may be established.'* [17] And if he refuses to hear them, tell it to the church. But if he refuses even to hear the church, let him be to you like a heathen and a tax collector.

Matthew 18:15-17 (NKJV)

Loving another person, again, is not negotiable, but allowing someone to continually abuse us is not required. Just be cautious. It is very simple to become self-righteous when accusing another. There are always three points of view: ours, theirs and God's. Only God sees the truth, as our point of view can be deluded. Notice that in the instructions of Jesus, we are to go to our brother. That is not an email or phone call, but a journey, and hopefully, while on that journey, we will have time to reflect on the situation. I remember a Christian brother who had hurt me deeply. After a few years, we finally got together, with a witness. The night before the meeting, I made a list of all the ways he had wronged me. I went to bed angry and woke up with a changed heart, the heart of grace. When we met, I felt sorry for this brother, rather than desiring accountability or punishment. All I did was offer him the same forgiveness that God had offered me! Having listened to my heart the day before, the witness really regretted suggesting the meeting, and then the next day, was joyous over God's change in my heart.

Finally, don't be the person who looks at others to find any evil or appearance of evil in their lives, and then spreads that gossip quicker than a forest fire. If all we did was look for sin in the lives of others, wouldn't it be just as easy for others to look for sin in our lives? Again, love covers a multitude of sins. If we are abiding in the Vine, and walking in God's *agape* love, then forgiving others will be a natural part of our walk. I held a grudge for so many years before I was a believer. I did not want to forgive, as I did not want to release the person who had hurt me from the bondage of what I thought they owed me. When I became a believer, and forgave them, I found that I had been the one in bondage. After forgiving, I walked in freedom for the first time, and it felt like the world I had been carrying on my shoulders was gone. Jesus' yoke is easy and His burden is light. If

119

you still feel that same bondage, holding hurt or slight against someone, let it go! We need to continually reassess if there is someone we need to forgive. Forgiveness is one of the greatest examples of God's love. How can we affect change without offering the same gift God has given us?

Chapter Six:
What the World Needs Now is Love!

One of the catch phrases of today's modern world is "celebrate diversity." Certainly, there are many different ethnicities, races, cultures, and religions surrounding us, and if that is not confusing enough, it seems that now we also can have different gender identifications along with different sexual orientation. Former Olympic decathlete Bruce Jenner, who claimed to always have identified as a woman, has now become Caitlyn Jenner, and even more perplexing, Caitlyn (just as Bruce was) is attracted to women. Bruce became a woman and a lesbian. Sounds like someone has a bruised gender! More children are being told that gender is a choice. My sister recently was on a hike and met a pregnant woman and her partner. "Are you having a boy or a girl," my sister asked. "We have decided to let the child choose which one it wants to be." Even with a world turning upside down, God commands us to love others.

For even though the times may have changed, God's Laws have not changed. Some people might look at His laws as archaic, or something that need to be updated. Yet God is outside of the confines of time, and His Laws do not need to change any more than He needs to change. Change does, however, need to occur in us. Jesus did update the 10 Commandments during His time on earth. As mentioned earlier, Jesus summarized those commandments, in response to the Pharisees once again trying to entrap Him. Here is that telling conversation:

> [34] But when the Pharisees heard that He had silenced the Sadducees, they gathered together. [35] Then one of them, a lawyer, asked *Him a question*, testing Him, and saying, [36] "Teacher, which is the great commandment in the law?" [37] Jesus said to him, " *'You shall love the Lord your God with all your heart, with all your soul, and with all your mind.'* [38] This is *the* first and great commandment. [39] And *the* second *is* like it: *'You shall love your neighbor as yourself.'* [40] On these two commandments hang all the Law and the Prophets."
> Matthew 22:34-40 (NKJV)

Certainly, none of God's commandments were unimportant, and failing to follow even one of those laws would make any man a sinner guilty of a death penalty. Yet Jesus summarized the 10 Commandments into only two. As mentioned earlier, if we love the LORD with all we have, we will obey the first four of the 10 Commandments. At the same time, if we love our neighbor in the way God calls for us to love, we will obey the last six of the 10 Commandments. We should not be surprised that the word "love" in these verses is *agape*. There is that unconditional love once again.

Loving others is the only way we can demonstrate how Jesus loves us. Just as Jesus drew us to Him by His love, that is what will draw others to Jesus, as well. If we judge others, rather than love them, that will create more separation. Our job as believers is to bridge the gap, not increase it. Many believers seem to cloister themselves. After all, Jesus reminded us to be in the world, but not of the world. Yet was He telling us to remove ourselves so far away that we actually are hiding? Picture a monk spending his life in silence, in a monastery far removed from others. Even if that monk has a deep love of God and knowledge of God, without loving others or sharing that love with others, what lives could he possibly touch? God does not rapture us to heaven the moment we accept Jesus as our Lord and Savior. Instead, He wants us to walk with Jesus while here, and in so doing, draw more people to the Lord. We cannot do that by sending our children to Christian schools, only associating with fellow believers, separating ourselves so distantly that our lives cannot witness to others, and come in close contact with others. This reminds me of the statement that we should not be so heavenly minded that we are no earthly good. At the same time, associating with non-believers does not mean that we need to compromise our beliefs.

Sometimes, it seems like all of life is a compromise. Compromise is defined as a settlement in which each side makes concessions. Lawyers spend hours negotiating compromises to ease time spent in litigation. One of the best biblical examples of compromise comes from the wisdom of King Solomon. Two harlots from the same house gave birth to children three days apart. When one of the newborn infants died in the night, the mother of that baby took the other woman's baby. Of course, she denied those claims. Solomon, gifted in God's wisdom, had to make a judgment though he was not there at the time. Notice that he did not condemn the women as harlots. After all, Solomon's great-great-grandmother was Rahab, also a harlot.

> And the king said, "Divide the living child in two, and give half to one, and half to the other."
> 1 Kings 3:25 (NKJV)

Of course, the thieving mother accepted that decision, as her baby already had died. Yet the actual mother revealed her honesty when she acknowledged that she would rather have the other mother raise the child than to see her child die. Solomon gave the true mother her child back. American news reporter Jane Wells said, "Learn the wisdom of compromise for it is better to bend a little than to break." That might be wisdom when it comes to settling differences within a

123

family or marriage, yet it is ignorance when it comes to compromising principles! Elbert Hubbard, a 20th-century American writer, had a different perspective when he said, "It's the weak man who urges compromise, never the strong man."

Our all-powerful God does not compromise. As God cannot change, getting involved in deal-making would demonstrate that He did not know what He was doing to begin with, which is definitely not the case. Additionally, we know that God always keeps His side of the bargain, which places cheaters on the other side of the bargaining table. When God makes a promise, we can take that covenant to the bank. Do our promises hold that same strength? As Christians, we face compromise on a daily basis. Do we compromise our integrity at work? Are our business ethics less defined than our ethics when dealing with fellow believers at church? "Everyone else does it," should not be an excuse, as we are not accountable to everyone else. Yet we are accountable to God. Do we compromise our Christian values when watching television, attending movies or even telling a dirty joke? Certainly, we all make mistakes. But God does not want us to compromise the Christian values He has given us. When the Lord calls us out of the world to serve Him, most of us walk away from behaviors that do not make us proud. Sadly, many people claiming to be Christians either continue in the old ways, or fall back into those old lives. Those compromises never work out well. In fact, when we compromise the Lord's calling on our lives, we are no better off than a baby cut in half! If there are compromises in our Christian walks, we should turn around and take a step back in God's direction. Otherwise, it is like a dog returning to its own vomit (Proverbs 26:11). As disgusting as it sounds, I am familiar with the feeling, unfortunately.

> For if, after they have escaped the pollutions of the world through the knowledge of the Lord and Savior Jesus Christ, they are again entangled in them and overcome, the latter end is worse for them than the beginning.
> 2 Peter 2:20 (NKJV)

If God has healed us and given us legs to walk, why would we choose to lose our legs again? When we choose the world, we choose Satan. When we choose God, our desire should be to obey Him, and through that obedience, demonstrate how much we love Him! God spoke directly to Joshua, who replaced Moses to lead the Jews after Moses' death, and encouraged Joshua to not compromise:

> Only be strong and very courageous; be careful to do according to all the law which Moses My servant commanded you; do not turn from it to the right or to the left, so that you may have success wherever you go."
> Joshua 1:9 (NASB)

With this clear language, there really is no "wiggle room." When it comes to God's Law, there is to be no compromise in the lives of believers. Veering slightly left or slightly right is still compromise, and in time, will lead us far from God's path. We can picture this easily with certain sins. Let's say that God rescued a man from drug addiction, and after walking clean for 10 years, the man starts believing he is strong enough to control the drugs that once controlled him. Nothing serious, just a little marijuana, is what he thinks. All of us know what will happen. It won't take long before this man is back in the same position he was before, broken. All sins are exactly the same, not just drug addiction. When God removes a sin from our lives, let it go! Sin is cancer that eats us from the inside out. We know that we should not play with matches, as we will get burned. How much more severe the burn is that comes from Satan when a believer compromises the calling God has on their lives! Satan has been using the same schemes for many years, and he is really good at getting believers to stumble. But God is stronger still, and we need to rely only on Him for our strength. Do not compromise, and that includes how we love others.

So how do we treat our gay neighbors, who invite us to a backyard barbecue? (I tend to focus a lot on that particular sin in many examples because I think the church in general seems to elevate that sin above all others. Part of this likely has to do with not being able to empathize with people choosing this sinful life, but again, sin is sin, and everyone needs redemption). Attending does not mean we need to get drunk with them, sleep with them or to hypocritically hide our Christian beliefs. Yet at the same time, we are not to condemn them, either. Only a judge is qualified to condemn, and as believers, God told us not to judge. Instead, we need to be listening to the Holy Spirit, looking for opportunities to share the love of Jesus. If the Holy Spirit opens the door, step through that door. Instead of telling them we cannot attend because we do not believe in their lifestyle, what if we attend and they ask us about our beliefs? Sounds like an open door to me, though when we speak, we need to choose our words carefully. When clothed in the love of Jesus and not in the condemnation of a self-righteous believer, those words might have an amazing effect. Yet even if we cannot see an immediate change, crops cannot be harvested until seeds are both planted and watered.

Agape love is not a spoken word, but an action verb! As discussed at length in the previous chapter, loving a person who loves us is a natural reaction, but God's calling on the hearts of believers is to love those who are not so easy to love. Jonah despised the Ninevites, and in each of our lives, we need to figure out who the Ninevites are. Some of the categories of people frequently mentioned are homosexuals, drug users, criminals and homeless people – the disenfranchised. What really is different about people in those categories to us? Do we think of their sins as more disgusting, or more egregious in the eyes of God? Are we really concerned that their sins offend God, or is it that we are personally offended instead? Pride can sometimes take us on interesting excursions, far from the intended destination. My sin stinks! It stinks so bad that without the work of Jesus on the cross, it earned me a death penalty. God did not choose me because of what I might accomplish as a Christian. He chose me to demonstrate His love. It does not matter what category a person falls into, they are just as redeemable as we are. Just as I did not earn the love of Jesus, and His love was a gift, we can share that same gift of God's love to others. The less they have earned that love, the more they need it. After all, God created all of us.

If we cannot logically deduce this ourselves, Paul does his best to help us:

> [7] Now therefore, it is already an utter failure for you that you go to law against one another. Why do you not rather accept wrong? Why do you not rather *let yourselves* be cheated? [8] No, you yourselves do wrong and cheat, and *you do* these things *to your* brethren! [9] Do you not know that the unrighteous will not inherit the kingdom of God? Do not be deceived. Neither fornicators, nor idolaters, nor adulterers, nor homosexuals, nor sodomites, [10] nor thieves, nor covetous, nor drunkards, nor revilers, nor extortioners will inherit the kingdom of God. [11] And such were some of you. But you were washed, but you were sanctified, but you were justified in the name of the Lord Jesus and by the Spirit of our God.
> 1 Corinthians 6:7-11 (NKJV)

Interesting. Even in the early church, all people had to do was to look around, see who was fellowshipping beside them, and they were able to identify people from all of these categories. God does not call the qualified, but qualifies the called. One of the key words in this passage from 1 Corinthians is "were," as it does not state, "and such are some of you," but "and such were some of you." In fact, almost every Christian falls into at least one of these categories. If we ever have placed anything in front of our relationship with God, we are guilty of idolatry, and are grouped with all of the people mentioned above. Why is it that we tend to see the sins of others as worse than our own sins? Paul certainly didn't see it that way, did he? He saw himself as the worst sinner ever to have lived. Man ranks sins, but God sees us all the way we really are…as sinners who can be redeemed by His grace, by the precious blood of the Lamb! God changes us. Moses was a murderer. King David also was a murderer and added adulterer to his list. Lest we forget, Jesus forgave one of the thieves on the cross near his last breath of life. That decision by Jesus certainly had nothing to do with the Christian life that the thief would lead from that day forward. Instead, that very day, the thief joined Jesus in paradise. As believers, most of us try to do our best, and try to follow the Lord. But loving others, especially those we cannot understand, is quite difficult. Jesus grouped us all together when he explained that a man with anger in his heart is guilty of murder, and a man who lusts is guilty of adultery. Yet even with that explanation, we try to place a "real murderer" or a "real adulterer" in a different category. What, or who, gives us the right? Certainly, God does not.

For a couple years, a very close friend with a homeless ministry encouraged me to attend a very legalistic church. He was trying to encourage both me and the pastor of the church at the same time. The pastor had such a genuinely soft heart for broken people, and though he had been raised with some legalistic beliefs, as a student of the Bible, he was doing his best to teach the congregation about grace. That congregation was steeped in the Law, thinking church attendance, baptism and tithing "earned" heaven. In addition, the pastor had such a soft heart for the homeless. He spent hours helping them, ministering to them, sheltering them, feeding them and teaching them about God and God's love. In addition, he allowed many to park their cars on church property. One of the things most of us do not understand about homelessness is that if living in a car, police will wake up anyone they find sleeping in the car and force them to move. Consequently, a night of good sleep is rare. It is almost impossible to stretch out in a car, so instead, they sleep for short periods, sitting. Just sleeping in a church parking lot became a blessing, but the blessings did not stop there. The pastor hired them for small jobs, and spent time with them. They had food to eat, too, and the pastor began to counsel each of them, ministering to their needs. He felt like he needed to give them time to heal, before expecting immediate results. They felt his *agape* love, and hearts began to change. When we pigeonhole people into categories, we miss out on their personal stories. One of the most important lessons I learned from both my friend and this pastor was to take the time to listen to each story, instead of judging them as a group. Each person is unique.

We draw conclusions, without knowing causes. Some of our conclusions are based on what we think to be true, or what may be true in many cases. For example, we surmise that all homeless people are mentally ill, or on drugs, or lazy. Let's say that a homeless

128

person is lazy, on drugs and mentally ill. Does that mean we should throw them away? Does it mean God does not love them? Does it mean we cannot improve their station in life simply by loving them? Maybe not, but we should at least try. This legalistic church finally had enough of the big-hearted pastor. Members of the church issued complaints to the city, that he was allowing people to sleep on the premises, claiming their concern was an insurance issue. Instead, most of us knew it was a heart issue with the people attending the church. It was the most joyless church I ever have experienced. Finally, they let the pastor go. Though it broke his heart, he was more concerned with how it would affect his homeless friends than how it affected him!

For the members of that church, the homeless people were the Ninevites. Those members would rather have seen each of those homeless people condemned to hell than to give them shelter in the church. The pastor had to protect his heart that the church congregation did not become the Ninevites of his life. We tend to forget that the Son of Man had no place to lay His head. It certainly sounds like Jesus was homeless. Would we judge Jesus as a loser for that reason alone?

Racism is another polarizing issue in our culture today. The "Black Lives Matter" campaign seems to demonstrate this great divide, with some thinking there is no problem, and others tired of the obvious discrimination they are subjected to. Personally, I think racism exists, and always will exist, this side of heaven. It is part of the human condition. Truly, there are not many people on this earth who do not look down on someone else. That is sin nature, and the sin of pride. A man with a $200,000 a year job may see his salary as something he has earned with hard work, not remembering the advantages of growing up in a household where needs always were met. Is the playing field level? Growing up in the south, I was a part of a powerful experiment. Instead of attending the nearby school, next door to a country club, a number of us were bussed across town to a black neighborhood school, West Charlotte High School. Many parents chose to send their children to private schools to avoid attending that school. Though it was a daily inconvenience for the additional miles traveled to school, the experiment was a huge success. In fact, schools from Boston, Massachusetts used West Charlotte as a model, dealing with the racism in that city. I learned huge lessons in those years. Regardless of culture or skin color, all of us are the same. My older sister remembers racial tensions, but I don't remember any. Perhaps I found more acceptance through participation on the athletic teams. But it changed me for life. Then I moved to Southern California, and most people in my small town claimed not to be racist. It is difficult to find a racist when everyone around is the same race. The existing racial divide in Southern California seems to focus on those of Hispanic heritage. Almost any time I passed a policeman issuing a citation, it was to a Hispanic man or woman.

Then, after 30 years, I returned to the South. Honestly, after what I experienced in high school, I expected the racial relations in Charlotte to have improved even more. Sadly, it may have gotten worse. As believers, shouldn't our churches be integrated, as we are serving the same God? To me, this is one of the most important areas for us to share our *agape* love with others. Do not fall into the trap of putting yourself above anyone else. God redeemed me, and all it takes is a good look into the mirror to know that if He saved me, He can save anyone. It starts with the basics. Look people in the eyes, with love in your heart and let them feel that love even if all you have to give is a greeting. Look for opportunities to bridge the gap. As believers, we need to be sensitive, and keenly aware, if we have allowed any racism to affect us. Think of a child who attends kindergarten with a diversity of other cultures. Does he come home and tell us about his black friend Anthony, or does he just talk about his new friend Anthony without identifying skin color? Without input, most children do not see race. Racism isn't innate, it is learned! When we start to see people as people and quit identifying them with names from the Crayola 64-pack, this will no longer be an issue. But again, this side of heaven, because of sin nature, racism will continue to exist.

In my first few months back in Charlotte, I spoke to everyone when entering and exiting the local grocery store, and noticed that many blacks would not even look at me. Before condemning, I realized that if we are constantly treated badly by one ethnicity, we can draw our own stereotypes. If all Caucasians had treated them badly, then rather than give me a chance, they stereotyped me. By moving to the other side of town, I saw completely different behavior, which made me think that racism still must be more prevalent on the other side of town.

God created all of us, and He certainly had a plan that included ethnic diversity. I can still remember relatives, who harbored hatred against other ethnicities while claiming to be Christians. My grandmother once showed me an article about her father after his death. He had been president of the Arkansas State Ku Klux Klan. In disgust, I asked for a copy of the article and she mistakenly said, "I knew you would be proud of him!" Seriously? I wanted that article because I never wanted to forget the evil that came from my ancestors. Certainly, in the name of his bigotry, he had murdered innocent people. The Bible speaks of an ancestral sin curse, that passes down through the generations. Interestingly, what removes that curse is a generation that loves the Lord. (See Exodus 34). Wasn't racism Adolf Hitler's driving force, his hatred of Jews? To attempt to destroy God's chosen people also points to Satanic influence. Once again, it is reflective of sin nature to pridefully elevate self and look down on anyone else.

Looking down on others does not have to involve genocide. For me, the greatest challenge seems to be while driving. There are so many horrible drivers. I feel myself stifling, "Idiot!" so often, and then God reminds me that everything I have is God-given. I have no right to compare myself to anyone else in any situation and think that I am better than they are. Again, look at the words in 1 Corinthians 13 for a reminder of aspects of *agape* love: patient and kind come to mind! In Luke's retelling of the statement of Jesus concerning the importance of loving our neighbors, a man asked Jesus to identify the meaning of that term "neighbor." Jesus answered by sharing a parable of the Good Samaritan:

[30] Jesus replied and said, "A man was going down from

131

Jerusalem to Jericho, and fell among robbers, and they stripped him and beat him, and went away leaving him half dead. [31] "And by chance a priest was going down on that road, and when he saw him, he passed by on the other side. [32] "Likewise a Levite also, when he came to the place and saw him, passed by on the other side. [33] "But a Samaritan, who was on a journey, came upon him; and when he saw him, he felt compassion, [34] and came to him and bandaged up his wounds, pouring oil and wine on *them*; and he put him on his own beast, and brought him to an inn and took care of him. [35] "On the next day he took out two denarii and gave them to the innkeeper and said, 'Take care of him; and whatever more you spend, when I return I will repay you.' [36] "Which of these three do you think proved to be a neighbor to the man who fell into the robbers' *hands*?" [37] And he said, "The one who showed mercy toward him." Then Jesus said to him, "Go and do the same."

Luke 10:30-37 (NASB)

To understand this story, we need a deeper insight into the term, "Samaritan." In the Old Testament, when God punished the northern tribes and they were taken into captivity by the Assyrians, and years later, the southern tribes became captives in Babylon, the land of Israel had a new population, albeit a small one. A small remnant of Israelites also remained. Samaria was one of the capitals of northern Israel, and Assyria's king sent people to live in Samaria, which was one of the capitals of northern Israel. These people worshipped idols and married some of the remaining Israelites.

[24] The king of Assyria brought *men* from Babylon and from Cuthah and from Avva and from Hamath and Sephar-vaim, and settled *them* in the cities of Samaria in place of the sons of Israel. So they possessed Samaria and lived in its cities. [25] At the beginning of their living there, they did not fear the Lord; therefore the Lord sent lions among them which killed some of them. [26] So they spoke to the king of Assyria, saying, "The nations whom you have carried away into exile in the cities of Samaria do not know the custom of the god of the

land; so he has sent lions among them, and behold, they kill them because they do not know the custom of the god of the land." [27] Then the king of Assyria commanded, saying, "Take there one of the priests whom you carried away into exile and let him go and live there; and let him teach them the custom of the god of the land." [28] So one of the priests whom they had carried away into exile from Samaria came and lived at Bethel, and taught them how they should fear the Lord. [29] But every nation still made gods of its own and put them in the houses of the high places which the people of Samaria had made, every nation in their cities in which they lived.
2 Kings 17:24-29 (NASB)

When the tribes returned from captivity, Samaria was populated by those who had intermingled idolatry of foreign gods with Judaism. Likewise, after the captivity, the returning Jews desired to follow the Lord, at least at the time. This added to the divide between these people. While the Samaritans thought of themselves as Jews, the Jews thought the Samaritans were lower than dogs. John 4:9 emphasizes that the Jews would have nothing to do with the Samaritans.

Obviously, Jesus did not feel this way, as He preached to the Samaritans! In the story of the Good Samaritan, notice the people who avoided the injured man – an Israelite priest and a Levite. Any man in either of those categories should have a deep understanding of God's Law, yet for both of those men, the Law was just words. In the Old Testament, God repeatedly reminded the Jews to treat strangers well. After all, they knew exactly what it felt like to be "strangers in a strange land." But these men familiar with the Old Testament scriptures only knew the words. Instead, the Samaritan walked the walk rather than just talking the talk. The Samaritan did all in his power to help the stranger, and note that because the stranger was from Jerusalem, was likely a Jew. Being a Jew, if awake, he probably would have hated the Samaritan. It would be interesting to know when the injured Jewish man recovered, if his disdain of Samaritans was gone, or if he continued to walk in racist superiority. We can see that even in the days of Jesus, racism existed.

While the Jews could expound upon all of their reasons for hating the Samaritans, just like racism today, that hatred was unfounded. Jesus chose that example specifically, as in so doing, He reminded us to love those who hate us. Most importantly, that kind of selfless love is action, not empty words. In addition, we should pay close attention to the example given by Jesus of a neighbor. A neighbor was not someone living in close proximity. In fact, the injured man likely never had met the priest, Levite or Samaritan. Instead, a "neighbor" is anyone who crosses our path in a given day! Do we stop to help change a flat tire, or at the very least, call AAA to make a stranger's bad day get a little better? Or do we follow the behavior of the priest and Levite? "It's not my problem." If we are not loving others in the way God commands, it is our problem. This Samaritan offered compassion to a stranger. Compassion is feeling someone else's pain. He also offered mercy. God has given us mercy and grace. Grace is getting something we have not earned, while mercy is not getting something we deserve. We do not deserve salvation, but through God's grace, He has given us salvation. We deserve death, and have earned it with our sinful lives, but through God's mercy, Jesus died for us. Showing compassion and mercy for others is *agape* love! God desires for us to give to others what He has given to us.

Racism points strongly to division, not unity. The player protests during the playing of the National Anthem at National Football League games either has increased this divide, or just called attention to it. Yet racism is not the only division. With a two-party system, our nation likely never has seen such a polarized division in all its history. There does not seem to be a majority, but split, completely down the middle. What has changed? Personally, I think there always have been contrasting opinions, and strength of conviction. But civility is gone. People seem unable to respectfully disagree, and instead, relationships are weakened, if not lost. One of my closest friends endured a complete split in his family over one vote. His gay brother-in-law supported John Kerry, the Democratic senator from Massachusetts in the 2004 presidential election, and stated that if anyone he knew did not hate George W. Bush, he never would speak to that person again. Sadly, those were not just empty words, as he actually cut people out of his life who did not only agree with his hatred, but emulate it!

Many Christians can be just as strong-willed in regard to politics. One pastor argued that every Christian would vote for the same candidate in every election, based on the unity of the Holy Spirit. What?! I reminded him that God's will would be done, regardless of how attentive I had been to the voice of the Holy Spirit. The Bible states that God appoints both countries and kings. In that passage, I do not see that statement qualified by saying, "if Garry is listening intently." If we were omniscient, as God, this would be different, but the last time I looked, that was not my superpower. Instead, God reminds us that we are citizens of heaven, not citizens of earth. We are just passing through. How often do travelers get involved in the politics of the land they are visiting? This does not mean that we should not vote, or take a stand. In Romans, Paul emphasizes that we are to follow the laws of the land, unless those laws conflict God's laws. Abortion is a perfect example. If God's Law commands us not to kill, and we proceed with an abortion because the laws of the nation allow it, we are still in violation of God's Law. Yet we still live in a broken world, under Satan's dominion, and consequently, we will continue to see brokenness. Hatred that accompanied slavery along with "accepted" racial bigotry existed openly until people finally stood up together, or sat down together in protest in the Civil Rights Movement. Though we as believers are to follow the laws of the land, we can take the legal steps to change laws. But once again, Paul's words do not give believers any wiggle-room, even when their most-desired candidate was not elected.

[1] Let every soul be subject to the governing authorities. For there is no authority except from God, and the authorities that exist are appointed by God. [2] Therefore whoever resists the authority resists the ordinance of God, and those who resist will bring judgment on themselves. [3] For rulers are not a terror to good works, but to evil. Do you want to be unafraid of the authority? Do what is good, and you will have praise from the same. [4] For he is God's minister to you for good. But if you do evil, be afraid; for he does not bear the sword in vain; for he is God's minister, an avenger to *execute* wrath

on him who practices evil. [5] Therefore *you* must be subject, not only because of wrath but also for conscience' sake. [6] For because of this you also pay taxes, for they are God's ministers attending continually to this very thing. [7] Render therefore to all their due: taxes to whom taxes *are due*, customs to whom customs, fear to whom fear, honor to whom honor.
Romans 13:1-7 (NKJV)

Paul's logic is solid. If God is in charge, and omnisciently places His chosen person to govern over us, then who are we to question God's choice? Obey the laws of the land, pray for those governing over us and accept that Romans 8:28 is still in the Bible. All things will work for the good of the believer and for the glory of God. Rather than arguing with people over differences of opinion, politically, maybe we should look for ways to love them.

Social media has made all of this increasingly difficult. Instead of open discussions, social media brings short quips and close-mindedness. Open-mindedness is how we learn. That same open-mindedness brought me to the Lord, as rather than thinking I had all the solutions, God used the brokenness in my life to remind me that doing it my way had caused the brokenness. Why not try it God's way, and see how that works? An open-mind does not mean that our mind will change, but by listening to someone with a different opinion, we may learn why they believe the way they do. Even by hearing them, and understanding them, we learn how to love them. For example, many of the people I have spoken with who claim to be atheists have adopted that belief because of the death of a close friend or relative. If God exists, then why would He allow that sadness, is the typical argument. Because of free will, and man's sinful choices, is God supposed to remove free will anytime the decision is a bad one, jolt them with a buzzer, like when playing "Operation?" We draw bad conclusions, and blame God for our choices. Death did not exist until man sinned. As believers, we need to have patience and thick skins. We can win half the battles just by listening, or in regard to social media, simply by not reacting. But just knowing someone else's point of view certainly gives us a great starting place in how to love them.

With discussions disappearing, social media also can offer anonymity, which increases bullying. By reading the comments with online news stories, a new level of hatred and nastiness exists. In years past, some of this hateful language would bring a punch in the nose, but the online bullies seem to relish in their ability to hurt or offend without recourse. What has happened to us? This is an easy question, and an equally easy answer. This nation was founded on God's principles, but we have removed God. Prayer is no longer allowed in the schools. Separation between church and state seems to emphasize a priority that has changed within our nation. We desire ease and financial prosperity, and even God's blessings, but we want those gifts without honoring God. "Merry Christmas" has become "Happy Holidays." As this nation no longer collectively and corporately worships God, changes have occurred throughout our culture. Certainly, the opioid crisis is another example of our removal of God. If we look to fill a void with heroin, instead of with God, what good do we expect to occur?

What do we see when we look around us? Racism, political divide, school shootings, drug abuse, hatred, failed marriages, single-parent families, latch-key children without any parental supervision or any love, the list goes on and on and on. What do these all have in common? Brokenness. I once was lost, but now am found. I once was blind but now I see. I once was dead, but am alive again! Jesus is the only answer, and the only way broken people ever will find Him as the answer is through our love. Love is action, not a feeling. It is a gift, not earned. If we remember how God's love changed us, we already know how to share that love with others – the same way God loved us!

Chapter Seven: Putting it all Together

Though there are many world religions, Christianity is much different than all of the rest. Take Islam, for example, where Mohammed wrote the Quran about himself. Instead, in Christianity, we see 66 books written by 40 different authors, all about Jesus. Christianity is neither the new age approach of finding spirituality in everything around us in an interconnected world, nor is it a religion. Instead, Christianity is a relationship, offered by our Creator. We are inter-connected, as God created all of us, but without that relationship to Him, abiding in the Vine, we are completely disconnected from Him. That relationship all comes down to love. Even non-believers are familiar with the most-quoted verse in the Bible, John 3:16:

> For God so loved the world that He gave His only begotten Son, that whoever believes in Him should not perish but have everlasting life.
> John 3:16 (NKJV)

Because God loved all of us so much, each person He ever created,

He gave us the opportunity for a relationship with Him. That relationship is not temporary, but permanent, but it is only through the love of Jesus. That love was sacrificial, and Jesus demonstrated how deep His love for us is with His willingness to leave heaven, to live a sinless life and to die a brutal death. We all know people who have difficulty even speaking the words, "I love you." Jesus not only shared those words, but lived those words, showing each of us willing to see a different kind of love. Love should change us – should change every aspect of our lives. In the same manner that Jesus placed the needs of others above the needs of self, He calls us to do the same.

> [3] *Let* nothing *be done* through selfish ambition or conceit, but in lowliness of mind let each esteem others better than himself. [4] Let each of you look out not only for his own interests, but also for the interests of others. [5] Let this mind be in you which was also in Christ Jesus, [6] who, being in the form of God, did not consider it robbery to be equal with God, [7] but made Himself of no reputation, taking the form of a bondservant, *and* coming in the likeness of men. [8] And being found in appearance as a man, He humbled Himself and became obedient to *the point of* death, even the death of the cross. [9] Therefore God also has highly exalted Him and given Him the name which is above every name, [10] that at the name of Jesus every knee should bow, of those in heaven, and of those on earth, and of those under the earth, [11] and *that* every tongue should confess that Jesus Christ is Lord, to the glory of God the Father.
> Philippians 2:3-11 (NKJV)

All we really need to do is to play, "Follow the Leader!" Jesus did not ask us to do what He says, not what He does. That would be hypocritical. Instead, He lived and died as an example, setting a standard for all of us to emulate. Jesus also realized that each of us would fall short of His standard, due to our sinful natures, and even knowing our failures, gave us a way of escape. Knowing what He has done for us, we have a calling on our lives, guidelines how to live. Our lives affect so many others. Drop a small pebble into a quiet lake and see how far the ripples go. Similarly, our lives will affect others we cannot see! Esteem others above self. This does not encourage us to put ourselves lower on the priority list. Instead, the true encouragement is to remove ourselves from the priority list. This kind of behavior is so contrary to the ways of the world, which emphasizes self above all else. If we take ourselves off the list, won't God still honor His promises of taking care of us as His children?

One world philosophy tells us that God helps them who help themselves. Sadly, some even claim that verse is in the Bible, but it is absent, and does not reflect the point of view of many other verses. God helps the helpless. He helps those who help others. When flying on a commercial airliner, if the airplane has an emergency in the air, oxygen masks drop from the compartment above. We would receive instructions to place our own masks on first before helping anyone else, like our children. Instead, God wants us to help others first. How interesting that this analogy has to do with oxygen, air. When Jesus returned to heaven, He promised to leave another Helper in His place, a Helper just like Him. That gift is the Holy Spirit, who indwells all believers. In Greek, the word for Holy Spirit is *pneuma* (πνεῦμα), which means air. In Hebrew, the word for Holy Spirit is *ruach* (רוּחַ), which also means air. Air is a perfect representation, to me. Though many people have great difficulty believing in something they cannot see, at the same time, they believe in air. Faith is not blind faith, as we can see the effects of our faith, just as we can see and feel the effects of air. If I take a deep breath of air, filling my lungs to capacity, and then dive into the ocean, swimming underwater, when the air runs out, I feel a sense of panic. Why? Well, I know what it feels like to have air in my lungs, and I also know what it feels like not to have air in my lungs. I need air to live, even though I cannot see it! Though some might argue the existence of God, I know God exists, and I know He loves me. How can I possibly know this? Just as I have experienced air, I also have experienced God. I know what it feels like not to have Him in my life, and I also know what it feels like to have Him in my life. I never want to be without Him again. Just before enduring the cross, Jesus prayed for His disciples, and all believers to come, with these words:

> And this is eternal life, that they may know You, the only true
> God, and Jesus Christ whom You have sent.
> John 17:3 (NKJV)

The Greek word for "know" used in this passage is *ginosko*
(γινώσκω), which is "knowledge by experience." Just as the
post-resurrection Jesus did not chastise Thomas for stating that he
must put his fingers into Jesus' nail-scarred hands to believe, God
realizes that most of us could come from the "Show-Me State."
Yet Jesus also reminded Thomas that blessed are those who believe
without seeing. We cannot see God's actions in our lives without
spiritual blinders being removed from our eyes. Before Jesus saved
us, we might have attributed His miracles to pure coincidence, but
after we have been changed by His love, we realize that there are
no such things as coincidences. God has a plan in each of our lives.
We know the end result, that He will continue to love us, guide us,
encourage us, protect us and dwell with us. But what He commands
us in those simple, two statements of the New Testament is: love
God and love others. Put God first. Put everyone else above us.
Simple statement, and it is a daily battle. You might argue, "If I put
everyone else above myself, who will take care of my needs? Who
will put a roof over my head, give me food, help me succeed?" God
will! This life has nothing to do with, "he who dies with the most
toys wins." Instead, this life is a trial, a proving ground. The most
important step of that trial is whether or not we choose to follow
Jesus.

Jesus is Messiah and Jesus is Lord, but those two statements are
not one in the same. As Messiah, Jesus saves us. From what? From
ourselves, mostly. We are dumb sheep, and frankly, most of our
decisions are not very wise. Jesus protects us from even our worst
decisions. He also saves us from eternal damnation. But after being
saved, the next step of realization is that Jesus is Lord. A Lord is
King, and rules and reigns. If Jesus is the Lord of our lives, He rules
and reigns over every aspect of our lives. What are we willing to
give Him? I always struggle in church when we sing, "I Surrender

All." This points to the biggest struggle of living in the world and not being of the world, as the Bible teaches. Every day, I seem to find new areas that I thought I had committed to the Lord, but held onto. I want to change the words of the song to, "I Surrender Some," "I Surrender Most," or "I Want So Badly to Surrender All." In Romans 12, Paul speaks of the "living sacrifice." Those words easily can apply to laying our lives down at the feet of Jesus, knowing that we must die to self and live for Him. Yet another aspect of that phrase is that many sacrifices we feel like we hand to Jesus, we take back from Him. Walk away from a sin in your life, and then find yourself sinning in that same way again. The sacrifice crawled off the altar and started breathing again. What should we do? Kill it again! Put it back on the altar. But also realize that it should not be much of a sacrifice to give up something that is dangerous to us, something that is killing us. Jesus wants us to have abundant life. That does not refer to financial prosperity, regardless of what televangelists might tell you. Jesus wants us to walk in fullness of joy, His joy.

We know that Jesus is the *Alpha* and the *Omega*, the first and the last. So let's start again with *Alpha*, the first letter of the Greek alphabet. Next, Jesus must become the Lord of our lives. The Hebrew word for Lord is *Adonai* (אֲדֹנָי). Then we begin to understand God's love for us, and it is a different kind of love, *agape*. This love is unconditional, sacrificial, without fail, enduring all. Most importantly, it is not earned, nor can it be. It is a gift, freely given. Once we know God's love for us, it encourages us to walk closely with Him, to abide in the Vine. That Vine is Jesus, and without a close connection to Him, our lives cannot, nor will not, bear any fruit. Jesus did not save us as a response to knowing what great things we would accomplish for Him. Instead, Jesus saved us regardless of our sin. Our good works, and the fruit of the Holy Spirit in our lives, are outward signs of the inward change. When we abide in Him, we rely on Him to lead our lives, and all we want to do with those lives is to glorify God. We can demonstrate our love for Jesus in response to His love for us through obedience. God's Word gives us the guidelines of what our lives should look like if we are abiding in Him. Next, we are in agreement with Him. That is *Amen*! Jesus is the *Amen*, it says in Revelation 3:14, the Faithful One. We also see 25 statements in the Gospel of John beginning with *"Amen, Amen,"* and each of them points to the authority of Jesus as God. In these statements, Jesus emphasizes some of the most important aspects of our lives as believers.

Finally, it comes back to *agape* love. After understanding God's love for us, and receiving His love in our lives, He calls us to love others. Who are we to love? Everyone! It doesn't take much to fall short of that calling, does it? Obviously, this kind of love is moment-by-moment, challenging and selfless. Who needs love the most? People who are unable to love others, or love us. One of the greatest reminders to each of us should be a reflection upon what our lives were like before we received God's love. How was He able to love me? If God can forgive me, how can I not forgive others?

Alpha
Adonai
Agape
Abide
Amen
Authority
Agape

Sometimes, prayer is the only way we can love others. Paul reminds us in Romans 12:18 that as believers, we are to be at peace with everyone, as much as possible. Regardless of what we do, there are people who will not be at peace with us. That makes it difficult to show them love, but the misbehavior of others does not affect what we do in private. We still can love them, grieve for them, and hope the best for them. And most importantly, we can pray for them. Prayer is perhaps the greatest and most powerful gift that God has given to believers. Personally, I tend to take the gift of prayer for granted far too often.

While writing this book, I have endured a great trial. I have neighbors with shared vents using drugs daily. Though I never have tried drugs, I was getting high daily, too. My sister Gwen asked if I had been praying for them, and I flippantly responded that I was praying for them to overdose. We may miss the irony that while writing a book on loving neighbors, I was having great difficulty loving my own neighbors. Was what they were doing wrong? Certainly, but that does not give me a release from the duty God has called me to perform.

> But I say to you, love your enemies, bless those who curse you, do good to those who hate you, and pray for those who spitefully use you and persecute you,
> Matthew 5:44 (NKJV)

God has given each believer access into His throne room, into the Holy of Holies. The Creator of the universe actually wants to hear from His children. Does He want to hear from unbelievers? There are numerous verses in the Bible that tell us that God does not hear the prayers of those who are not His! Just as only the sheep of Jesus hear His voice, it would seem that the Good Shepherd only hears the voices of His sheep. There is one exception. God always hears the salvation prayer of an unbeliever, for when that heart desire changes from the cares of the world to wanting to follow Jesus, God is willing to forgive. Let's look at some of these verses:

> "We know that God does not hear sinners; but if anyone is God-fearing and does His will, He hears him.
> John 9:31 (NASB)

> He who turns away his ear from listening to the law,
> Even his prayer is an abomination.
> Proverbs 28:9 (NASB)

> For the eyes of the Lord are toward the righteous,
> And His ears attend to their prayer,
> But the face of the Lord is against those who do evil."
> 1 Peter 3:12 (NASB)

> The Lord is far from the wicked,
> But He hears the prayer of the righteous.
> Proverbs 15:29 (NASB)

23 "Turn to my reproof,
Behold, I will pour out my spirit on you;
I will make my words known to you.
24 "Because I called and you refused,
I stretched out my hand and no one paid attention;
25 And you neglected all my counsel
And did not want my reproof;
26 I will also laugh at your calamity;
I will mock when your dread comes,
27 When your dread comes like a storm
And your calamity comes like a whirlwind,
When distress and anguish come upon you.
28 "Then they will call on me, but I will not answer;
They will seek me diligently but they will not find me,
29 Because they hated knowledge
And did not choose the fear of the Lord.
Proverbs 1:23-29 (NASB)

This last one quoted seems harsh, almost mocking. Yet we also know that God created everyone, and has given everyone the opportunity to know Him. If we choose not to know Him, not to acknowledge Him, then it seems pretty ridiculous to think that we can use God for an advantage only when life is difficult. Like I said before, we have a tendency of blaming God for difficulties and taking personal credit for successes. When the child of an unbeliever dies and the unbeliever blames God, how did that become God's fault? Many have a misconception of God playing games with our lives. If we do something good, then He will love us more, or give us a reward. On the other hand, if we do something bad, we expect a slap on the hand or a jolt of electricity to remind us we did wrong. But we are not hamsters on a great hamster wheel in the laboratories of a mad scientist named God. Nor are we pawns on a cosmic chessboard. God loves us. He wants all of us to know Him and love Him. But if we are not God's children, then even in the midst of calamity, He does not hear those prayers.

That encourages me, rather than discourages me, as it deepens my purpose. For if God does not hear the prayers of the unsaved, but He hears my prayers, He certainly will listen to my prayers when my unsaved friends and unsaved family members are hurting. Especially in regard to prayers for the unsaved, the focus of our prayers should not just be on momentary relief, but on permanent relief through their salvation! Love others through actions, love others through words and love others through prayers.

> [12] "Truly, truly, I say to you, he who believes in Me, the *works* that I do, he will do also; and greater works than these he will do; because I go to the Father. [13] "Whatever you ask in My name, that will I do, so that the Father may be glorified in the Son. [14] "If you ask Me anything in My name, I will do *it*. [15] "If you love Me, you will keep My commandments.
> John 14:12-15 (NASB)

Reflect on the miracles Jesus performed, and in this statement, Jesus promises that we will accomplish more than He did. How is that possible? As believers, we are one body. Collectively, we can go to the far reaches of the world. Even if all God required of each believer was to love one other person, imagine the number of lives that would change! Yet God wants us to wake up each and every day, and understand that each person He places in front of us is not an accident or coincidence. That person is a ministry! Love them, the way Jesus loves us.

Beloved (those special people deeply loved by God with His *agape* love), be loved. Receive that love. Then love others with God's *agape* love.

Beloved, Be LOVED!

Acknowledgments:

One night in my Bible study small group, we discussed how most men do not have a close, male, Christian friend. Women seem to be better at this, perhaps because their hearts seem to be a little softer. Maybe part of the difficulty for men is that by showing our weaknesses to another, we feel less powerful, less in control. Yet with God in control, that openness or transparency with another can give us an important second voice. At one time in my Christian walk, I saw it as myself and Jesus alone, but this is not the Garden of Eden. Instead, I live in a world populated by other people. Those people have impact on my life, just as I am to have an impact on theirs. I seemed to be in the minority in my small group, as I have three incredibly close friends, strong believers. Each of them has made a deep impact on my life. Hopefully, they would say the same about me.

First, I would like to acknowledge Jeff Kirst. This book really began with a study years ago on John 15 and the Vine. Jeff invited me to a Bible study. At the time, I was in a "poor me" mode, having endured a really difficult church split. In addition, I was struggling financially and blamed it on God. But the decisions that put me in that place were mine, not God's. After months of complaining, I finally put the struggle in the rearview mirror. I had been reviewing all God's promises in the Bible, and realized that if I chose not to believe God, I was calling Him a liar. Ashamed, I asked for His forgiveness for my months of mistrust, and was looking to find fellowship again. I attended the study and frankly, it was a bit of a mess. In the discussions, men were using the foulest language, including one of the leaders. In a Bible study! Jeff actually expected me not to come back, but God had opened a door. I was going to step through it. One of the two leaders died that week. Within weeks, the other leader wanted to step down and asked me to lead. We were studying some Christian books, but reading the books, I could see some incorrect biblical interpretation. Jeff saw the same, and each of us came to the same conclusion without prodding from the other. I decided to teach an inductive Bible study on John 15, which was the subject of one of the books we were reading. In addition to learning about John 15, each person could learn how to study the Bible, and see God's interpretation, rather than having that interpretation clouded by preconceived notions.

"Abide" became a focus for both of us for a long time. Last year, Jeff started studying "*agape*" very deeply. Though I live 3,000 miles away, we still spend hours on the phone discussing the Bible, and discussing the issues of our lives. Geography cannot remove closeness. It makes me think of Paul leaving the churches of different cities. His heart was saddened for the people he would miss, but even though God placed new people in Paul's path, the dear ones never lost their places in his heart. Thanks, Jeff, for the years of deep friendship, your biblical wisdom and the encouragement to keep writing. Jeff also read the book in advance of publication, looking for errors!

Dave Rann is another dear Christian brother. Everything I have done in ministry, Dave has supported. That includes financially, but most importantly, I never have felt like I was alone on the front of the battle lines. We have tennis in common and have spent many hours in fellowship together. More a brother than a friend, I have shared the depth of my struggles with him, all without any judgment. With Dave and I both working full time, and the time difference between the East and West coasts, we no longer get to speak as often as both would like. Again, this is one of the disadvantages of moving 3,000 miles across the country. But nothing could harm this friendship. One of the most difficult aspects of the move was leaving a place where I had many close Christian friends and moving to a place where I did not have any. Dave encouraged me to find a Bible Study Fellowship group, and that has been a huge blessing. Dave, thanks for the years of support. I have learned much about *agape* love by watching you. When I think of Dave, I think of a man of God who always puts Jesus first in his life. What an example to follow!

Finally, Todd Williams also has impacted my life in the deepest ways. For years, I walked far away from God, and at one time, professed to be an atheist. Todd never quit. I cannot tell you the number of 12-page letters I received from Todd over the years, in the days before email. In each letter, Todd responded to my questions, not flippantly. Nor did he expect me to know the Christian answer. Instead, Todd spent time and energy trying to feel what I was feeling. His compassionate spirit never judged me, nor did he ever stop loving me. And yes, in each letter, Todd kept telling me about Jesus. One day, I finally decided to give Jesus a chance. Likely, all of us as believers have a person who made the greatest impact on our salvation. Of course, the Holy Spirit draws us, but God certainly uses people to share His love with others. Todd is that person in my life, and it did not stop with my salvation. I'd like to think that I have been a special ministry for Todd, but I think he has impacted many people in the same way he has impacted me. Love in action!

Jeff, Dave and Todd, thanks from the bottom of my heart. There is nothing I would not do for any of you. I know much more about *agape* love after receiving it from you! All three of these men would not be the same without their supportive, loving, Christian wives, so thanks also to Kathy Kirst, Barbara Rann and Denise Williams. I would like to offer a special thanks to Denise, who read the first draft of this book with the keen eye of an editor, and also the soft heart of a mature Christian. Denise, your part in this began in your kitchen on the day I felt God's prodding to write it! There are others, too numerous to mention, who continue to impact me. Do not be offended if I have left you out, as if the list were all-inclusive, you could double the size of this book. But thanks to Tom Thorne, John Begin, Anthony Herron, Dan Archer and Rick Emory, too.

Of course, no acknowledgment would be complete without pointing to Jesus, my Savior and Lord. He came to me, right where I was, in the midst of sin, loved me, forgave me, and began to teach me how to love others. I have so much more to learn, but Jesus has promised to complete His work in me. This book is all about Him! May God be glorified.

Other Books by Garry Glaub:

"Here Am I! Send Me." A Commentary on the Book of Isaiah
(Volume I: Chapters 1-23)
ISBN 978-1-6047741-0-8 (442 pages) 2007

To God Be the Glory Daily Devotional
ISBN 978-0-9847533-0-7 (803 pages) 2011 (Hardcover)
ISBN 978-0-6155492-7-9 (803 pages) 2011 (Softcover)

Throughout Your Generations, A Christian Seder
ISBN 978-0-9847533-1-4 (76 pages) 2013

Strength & Beauty, The Book of Ruth
ISBN 978-0-9847533-2-1 (113 pages) 2014

The Shoes of the Jews, A 7-Week Bible Study on Enduring Trials
ISBN 978-0-9847533-3-8 (125 pages) 2014

40 Days Through the Gospels (Chronologically with the NLT)
ISBN 978-0-9847533-9-0 (400 pages) 2015

You can email Garry at:
gg4jesus@gmail.com

More information available at
www.garryglaub.com

or Garry's YouTube channel:
gg4jesus

Garry is available for weekend retreats to teach the importance of understanding and receiving God's *agape* love, abiding in the Vine, and pouring that love into the lives of others!